FFIRMING
FAITH

United Church Press
Cleveland, Ohio

FFIRMING
FAITH

a confirmand's journal

United Church Press, Cleveland, Ohio 44115

© 1996 by United Church Press

Biblical quotations are from the New Revised Standard Version of the Bible,
© 1989 by the Division of Christian Education of the National Council of
the Churches of Christ in the U.S.A., and are used by permission

Printed in the United States of America on acid-free paper

05 04 03 02 01 00   10 9 8 7 6

Project developers: Grant F. Sontag and Gordon J. Svoboda II

Project consultant: R. Kenneth Ostermiller

Project editor: Kathleen C. Ackley

Contributors: Kealahou Alika, Elizabeth Bassham, William Koch

Affirming Faith: A Congregation's Guide to Confirmation, ISBN 0-8298-1065-X

Affirming Faith: A Confirmand's Journal, ISBN 0-8298-1066-8

CONTENTS

WELCOME

Welcome to *Affirming Faith: A Confirmand's Journal*. This journal is your guidebook for the confirmation journey, giving you helpful background information, scriptures, stories, and prayers; asking you some important questions; and providing space for you to write, draw, doodle, and reflect about God and faith.

The section called "Before You Gather" gives you some background for each session. The section called "Questions to Consider" has questions for you to think about alone, in your group, or with a mentor.

You will need to bring your journal to each session, retreat, or time with your mentor. However, you will be asked to share only what you want, and you do not have to show your journal to anyone else. Be honest. Put in it whatever you want. It is for your questions, your doubts, your affirmations, your joys, and your prayers.

Keep your journal for future reference. It contains information that you will find helpful now and in the months and years to come. It can be fun to look back at what you were thinking, doing, and feeling during this time of your faith journey, preparing for the rite of confirmation.

May God's grace and love be with you on this exciting journey!

Our story as the
people of
God is con-
tained in
Scripture, in
Christian
communities,
and in the
lives of
individual
Christians.

AFFIRMING  faith

COMMUNITY LIFE

ON A FAITH JOURNEY

Prayer Is . . .

Prayer is the best way to get the personal depth of religious insight before which your doubts will flee away.
—Georgia Harkness

Prayer is the language of the Christian community.
—Henri Nouwen

Prayer is yearning, beseeching, and beholding.
—Julian of Norwich

Prayer is acknowledging that we are always in the presence of God.
—Bishop Desmond Tutu

Prayer is a force as real as terrestrial gravity.
—Alexis Carrel

What Do You Think?

@   If you were asked to explain prayer to someone, what would you say?

_____

_____

_____

_____

@   What does prayer mean to you?

_____

_____

_____

_____

@   Can you recall a time when you or someone else you know prayed? What was that like?

_____

_____

_____

_____

@   Some people think praying is only for asking God for something. What other purposes are there for prayer?

_____

_____

_____

_____

Some Elements of Prayer

@ PRAISING

@ GIVING THANKS

@ ASKING

@ LISTENING

The Prayer of Our Savior

"Jesus was praying in a certain place, and after he had finished, one of his disciples said to him, 'Teach us to pray, as John taught his disciples'" (Luke 11:1). So Jesus taught his disciples what was to become the most known and often recited prayer in the church today. Here are two versions of the Prayer of Our Savior. There are other versions as well.

Our Father in heaven,

    hallowed be your name,

    your kingdom come,

    your will be done,

    on earth as in heaven.

Give us today our daily bread.

Forgive us our sins

    as we forgive those who sin against us.

Save us from the time of trial

    and deliver us from evil.

For the kingdom, the power,

    and the glory are yours

    now and forever. Amen.

Our Father-Mother, who is in the heavens,

    may your name be made holy,

    may your dominion come,

    may your will be done,

    on the earth as it is in heaven.

Give us today the bread we need;

    and forgive us our debts,

    as we have forgiven our debtors;

    and do not put us to the test,

    but rescue us from evil.

For yours is the dominion, and the power,

    and the glory forever. Amen.[1]

---

1. *The New Century Hymnal* (Cleveland, Ohio: The Pilgrim Press, 1995), 56–57. Used by permission.

Dear Confirmand,

What does it mean to you to go on a journey? Would you look at the calendar and decide the best time to go? Would you set out on your own or wait for an invitation from others to go? Would you feel the excitement building as the day to begin approaches? Would you think about the things you will need on the journey and make a list? Would you be eager to have companions to go with you?

Journeys can be exciting and fun. Getting ready for confirmation is like going on a journey. Growing in faith and learning about God can be a journey—a journey of faith.

This time may mark the beginning of your journey with God. Or your journey with God may have started much earlier. In any case, an invitation to journey on from where you are now is what *Affirming Faith* is all about. God meets you right where you are—understanding your thoughts, your feelings, your questions, your affirmations—and calls you to begin this exciting journey.

Sincerely,

Your friends in Christ

Your friends in Christ

P.S. Have fun making a "time capsule" of your hopes for this journey. You will be able to open it at the end of the confirmation process.

Your Thoughts

_____

_____

_____

_____

_____

_____

_____

_____

_____

_____

_____

_____

_____

_____

_____

_____

_____

_____

_____

_____

_____

SHARING OUR STORIES

1

Themes

- Our story as the people of God is contained in scripture, in Christian communitites, and in the lives of individual Christians.
- We are to "go and tell" our faith story.
- By sharing our stories, we discover our connections to other followers of Jesus.

Scriptures

MATTHEW 28:1–20—Jesus appears to Mary Magdalene and the other disciples.

LUKE 8:1–3—Women and men go with Jesus to bring good news.

Before You Gather

The Christian story can draw us in and change us in amazing ways. By hearing about others—their faith and doubts, their encounters with God, and what it means for them to live life as Christians—we become part of the story too. We want to know a loving God who understands us and accepts us as we are. We want to have a connection to God and with others through Jesus Christ. We want to become part of the vision of the reign of God. As we become engaged in the story, we become part of it.

Our experience with the Christian story comes from at least three different places when we are part of Christian community: the Bible, the worshiping congregation, and the witness of Jesus' followers throughout history to the present. When the good news of the story is told, lives may be transformed and God's love may be known.

When we look to the Bible, we discover the story of our relationship with God. There we find the history of salvation: how we, as God's people, go through cycles in our covenant (promises we make) with God, failing to live up to our promises to be faithful, often by forgetting God and worshiping false gods. When we realize our failure and repent—have a change of heart, mind, attitude, and habit—God's mercy and forgiveness are ours. The covenantal relationship with God is based on the promise that God is our God and we are God's people. The Bible is our primary source for this story. It tells us what kind of people we are as the people of God.

The worship life of a congregation is another important source for the retelling and remembering of our story. Through the prayers, praise, proclamation of the Word, and sharing of the sacraments, worship is a joyful response of God's people to God's redeeming love in Christ. The whole Christian year, with its seasons, colors, symbols, and holy days, helps to tell the life of Christ—the central figure in our story. This is especially true when the *Revised Common Lectionary*, a three-year cycle of scripture readings, is used in worship. Each cycle is centered on one of the Synoptic (story-sequenced) Gospels (Matthew, Mark, and Luke). Texts from the Gospel of John are spread over all three years. The readings follow a sequence that is intended to lead worshipers to a deeper understanding of Christ's life, death, and resurrection and encourage a faithful response to God's saving grace.

We also need to share the Christian story as it has been lived out in history and is being lived today. We need to hear the stories of children, youth, and adults of all ages. We need to hear the testimonies of people who are different from us, who are from different cultures, or who have different abilities. We need to be open to the witness and movement of the Holy Spirit in our lives and in the lives of others. Being part of a faith community with people who are willing to share their faith helps to remind us of the covenantal relationship God seeks to have with us. It guides us into the future. Hearing the stories of people of faith gives richness and dimension to our story and helps us to find our identity as followers of Christ. It help us to appreciate the diversity in our own local church and the Christian church as a whole.

Hearing scripture, worshiping together, sharing personal faith stories, and hearing the stories of others whom we may never meet face to face helps us to believe that God loves each of us and will work in our lives too.

Life Line

Mark on the life line the significant events that are part of your life history. They can include events such as your birthday, when you started school, when you learned a new skill, met an important friend, faced losses, and so forth.

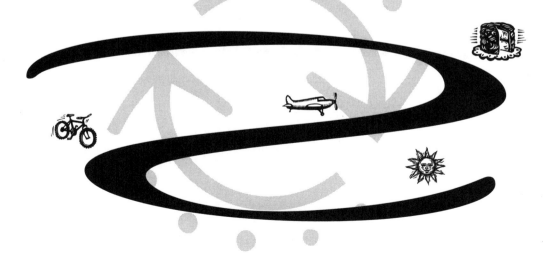

Questions to Consider

@ What are some of the times when you have been aware of God's presence with you?

_____

_____

@ What experiences, events, or people have helped you to know of God's presence?

_____

_____

@ How have your family, friends, or members of the church helped you in your faith journey?

_____

_____

@ What qualities or traits might someone else see in you that show your faith?

_____

_____

@ What qualities or traits do you hope God will help you develop as your faith grows?

_____

_____

@ Even though our faith journeys and experiences are unique, have you discovered ways your story connects to the stories of others?

_____

_____

God's People Tell Their Stories[1]

One group of youth preparing for confirmation wrote to leaders of the United Church of Christ asking, "Why do you believe in God, and why are you a disciple of Jesus Christ?" They also asked for words of encouragement as they prepared for confirmation. Here are some of the responses. Read them and answer the questions that follow.

My own faith journey began just as yours, when I was a teenager in a United Church of Christ in Massachusetts. Even as a young person, I knew that I needed God to be a powerful presence in my life. As an African American, life was not always easy for me in the suburban community where I grew up. I knew that I could not "go it alone" in my daily journey. Jesus became an important figure for me, because he, too, was not always at the center of the "in group" even though the crowds always wanted to hear him speak. He had a powerful relationship to God which sustained him through many trials and tribulations. His love and compassion for people became a window for me of how embracing God's love really is for all creation. During this time, Dr. Martin Luther King came to my church. He preached that God's love and the protective power of Jesus were so strong that people of hate and meanness could not stamp out such love even with police dogs and billy clubs. I learned to my amazement that to stare hate in the face with love and with the belief that God's spirit would transform the world and create more peace and justice erased fears and made my soul stronger. That's how I became a member of the United Church of Christ. The memory and awareness of God's amazing Grace in the face of adversity and today's troubles, keeps me in the church and from being overwhelmed by the problems of the world.

—Valerie Russell, Executive Director,
Office for Church in Society, United Church of Christ

God is very real to me. I do not understand everything about God, but I do know that God loves the world and all of us who are a part of it. God gives us the choice of whether or not we will accept God's love. If we do, some wonderful things happen. We love God in return and love our neighbor as ourselves. God's Spirit gives us the courage and strength to love others, even when it is not an easy thing to do.

—William A. Hulteen Jr., Executive Director and Minister for the Office of Church Life and Leadership, United Church of Christ

I *know* God because I have experienced so many times when I have been sustained in the midst of life's most difficult situations by a lightness of feeling I neither understand nor question. I am a *disciple* of Jesus, the Christ, because his way is the way I have chosen to live and respond to God's gift of life. I encourage you to keep asking questions and to follow your doubts as well as your beliefs about what it means to be Christian.

—Carole Gerhardy-Keim, Interim Conference Minister, Hawaii Conference, United Church of Christ

When I was confirmed we learned about our faith by memorizing a set of questions and answers about God and the church. The first question was, "What is your only comfort in life and in death?" The answer we learned was, "That I belong, body and soul, in life and in death, not to myself, but to my faithful savior, Jesus Christ." Faith means that no matter what happens in life, we belong to Jesus. And because we belong to Jesus, we belong to all other Christians in the church and reach out to all people everywhere. With God, you and I are always included and loved.

—Paul H. Sherry, President, United Church of Christ

I believe in God because I can do no else. It is clear to me through my own prayer life and as I work pastorally with other people that God is present and active in our world. I am a disciple of Jesus Christ because in Jesus I see one who has experienced and who teaches about

God's presence. I certainly encourage you as you prepare for confirmation. You will in the course of your life face a variety of challenges. You will find people who love you and people who hate you. You will face death and sadness. You will see injustice in the world. An unexamined faith is not worth having. An examined faith is worth more than life itself. An examined faith is one that gives you a foundation for your life and your living.

—Lynne S. Fitch, Conference Minister,
Washington North Idaho Conference, United Church of Christ

This is a very scary, hard thing to be a Christian. Jesus said that if we would follow him, we must pick up our cross. So maybe I should give a word of warning. But the only really important thing in life is to be at this task of forming a meaningful, inclusive human loving community. You will have to struggle all the way, but God will sustain you in the struggle.

—Jay Lintner, Director, Washington Office,
Office for Church in Society, United Church of Christ

When I was in high school I was a very bitter, angry, skeptical person. Like a lot of other people my age, I wasn't very happy about myself or anything else. Then one day as I was walking down to the bus stop, I got a message that wasn't really verbal, but which communicated the message, "It's ok. You are all right. You are very much loved and cared for." That changed my whole outlook about being alone in this universe. As I grew I also learned that Jesus is the Good News of God's love for everyone, everywhere. And that living life the way Jesus shows us is the way to a worthwhile life that is full of joy and meaning and wonder. Please remember that confirmation is the first step in your lifelong adventure of spiritual learning and growth.

—Armin L. Schmidt, Executive Director, Council for
American Indian Ministry, United Church of Christ

God has claimed my life because God is more true than any truth I know, any love that is possible, and any power that matters. As you prepare for confirmation, please trust the truth and wonder, the power and love of Jesus' life and death and living presence among us. And I encourage you to live that trust out in the church which is the community of that faith.

—Ansley Coe Throckmorton, President, Bangor Theological Seminary

When I was eight years old, I made a commitment to be a Christian. I gave my life to Jesus Christ then and was baptized. I gave my life to Jesus because I believed that Jesus would take away my sin and make me whole. I still believe that. Jesus has always led me to God. When sometimes God seems distant, it is because of Jesus that I feel God's presence within me. Confirmation is not the end of your Christian pilgrimage. It is just the beginning. Always remember that you are a child of God.

—David Y. Hirano, Executive Vice President, United Church Board for World Ministries, United Church of Christ

@ How would you answer the questions posed by the confirmation group: "Why do you believe in God, and why are you a disciple of Christ?"

_____

_____

_____

_____

_____

_____

_____

_____

_____

_____

_____

_____

◉ In the stories from others, what words were most helpful?

_____

_____

_____

_____

_____

_____

_____

◉ Encouraging?

_____

_____

_____

_____

_____

_____

_____

◉ Surprising?

_____

_____

_____

_____

_____

_____

_____

_____

Prayer

God, help me be open to the ways my faith can change and be strengthened when I hear others' stories. Help me to think about my own faith story and where it will take me. Amen.

Your Thoughts

_____

_____

_____

_____

_____

_____

_____

_____

_____

_____

_____

_____

_____

_____

_____

_____

_____

_____

1.   Quotations used by permission of the authors.

WORSHIP

2

Themes

@ Worship is the way God's people offer praise and thanksgiving to the living God.

@ Worship is the way God's people respond to God's grace and God's initiative in our salvation.

@ Worship gives order to the church's life, linking the past to the present and the future.

@ Worship is not limited to any particular place or time.

Scriptures

JOHN 4:21–24—True worship may happen anywhere if we worship God in spirit and truth.

PSALM 100—Worshipers are called to praise God in joyful celebration.

ACTS 2:22–42—Peter speaks of God's saving love through Jesus Christ.

ACTS 10:34–48—Peter preaches to the Gentiles and many receive the gift of the Holy Spirit and are baptized in Christ's name.

Before You Gather

Think of an average Sunday service of worship at your church. What happens during that time? What comes to your heart and mind? Problems? Fears? Friends?

Concerns for the world and its people? Do you ever imagine what God is like or how God thinks? Do you wonder what you are supposed to do with your life as a follower of Christ?

Worship practices throughout Christ's church reflect the church's diversity and often defy definition. Yet worship is one of the best and most effective ways to renew our faith and form our ideas about what it means to be a Christian.

Think of your worship experience; how much of it do you connect with a particular day, time, group of people, or place? For example, you might think of worship on Sunday morning, in your local church, surrounded by people you know.

So often when we think of worship, our thoughts are too limited. We may envision only that one hour, on Sunday, surrounded by those familiar faces. But worship can happen anywhere, anytime, in a group of any size. The possibilities and situations for worship to occur are endless—from singing songs to God on a wooded hillside to gathering with others at work or play to pray, praise, and thank God.

The word *worship* actually comes from the old English word *weorthscipe—weorth*, which means "worthy," and *scipe*, which means "ship."[1] The combination of words refers to the way we place worth and value on things and persons. While a service of Christian or Jewish or Muslim worship assumes that it is God who is the one we give value and worth to above all, it is important to remember that we can worship almost anything, as the Israelites did with the golden calf and as we do with all kinds of things. Another word used often, *liturgy*, comes from the ancient Greek and means literally "the people's work."[2]

Within the United Church of Christ, worship may take many forms and occur in a variety of places with groups of any size; but its purpose is still to provide us with the opportunity to praise and give thanks to God, our Creator, Redeemer, and Sustainer. This is our task as God's faithful people.

The Church Year[3]

Through the course of a year, the story of the birth, life, death, and resurrection of
Jesus Christ; the gift of the Holy Spirit; and the birth of the Christian church
are reflected in the seasons of the church. The church year and the use of the
Revised Common Lectionary underscore for a worshiping congregation the saving
acts of God as told in Hebrew and Christian Scriptures.

By the end of the fourth century C.E., the following seasons of the church year
were observed:

ADVENT (blue or purple)

This season centers on preparing for the anniversary of Christ's birth. It also antici-
pates Christ's return at the close of history. Advent consists of four Sundays—
the first Sunday in Advent is observed four Sundays prior to December 25.
Many churches and families observe this season with the lighting of Advent
candles. A new candle is lit each Sunday as a sign of the growing anticipation
of Christ's birth. The third Sunday is traditionally known as Gaudete Sunday,
the day of joy (this candle can be pink). A fifth candle, usually white, symbol-
izing Christ, is lit on Christmas Eve or Christmas Day.

CHRISTMAS (white)

The season of Christmas marks the celebration of God's coming to us in the person
of Jesus. It is twelve days long and continues until Epiphany, January 6. Christmas, the festival day of the birth of Jesus, is celebrated on December 25. In the
Roman calendar this was the date of the winter solstice. By the fourth century
C.E., the church had transformed the day to celebrate and honor the one who
came to be the Light of the World.

EPIPHANY (white and green)

Epiphany, which means "to show," is observed on January 6. The focus of this day, and the Sundays following, is Jesus as God's gift to the world, emphasized by the visit of the Magi (Matthew 2:1–12). Other stories traditionally a part of this season are Jesus' baptism (Matthew 3:13–17, Mark 1:4–11, Luke 3:15–16, 21–22) and Jesus' transfiguration (Matthew 17:1–9, Mark 9:2–9, Luke 9:28–43).

LENT (purple; Ash Wednesday—black; Palm/Passion Sunday—red; Maundy Thursday—white; and Good Friday—black)

Lent is the season that focuses on self-examination, prayer, and fasting in preparation for Holy Week. The name *Lent* comes from the word "to lengthen" and is associated with the spring of the year and increasing length of the daylight hours. Lent begins on Ash Wednesday and lasts forty days (not counting Sundays), ending on Easter Sunday. The observance of Ash Wednesday may include a special worship service, involving the call to a Lenten discipline, the marking of the forehead with ashes, and the remembrance of one's baptism.

Lent concludes with Holy Week, which includes:

@ Palm/Passion Sunday—remembering Jesus' entrance into Jerusalem for the observance of Passover and the beginning of his Passion

@ Maundy Thursday—remembering Jesus' last meal with his disciples, his washing of their feet as a call to ministry, and the giving of the new commandment (*mandatum*) to love one another (John 13:34-35)

@ Good Friday—remembering the crucifixion and death of Jesus Christ

EASTER (white)

Easter Sunday and the season that follows celebrate Christ's victory over death. In the early church, a worship service called the Easter Vigil began Saturday night of Holy Week and lasted until dawn of Easter morning, announcing the wonderful news of Christ's resurrection. The Easter season is the most joyful one in the church year.

PENTECOST (red; Sundays following—green)

The fiftieth day after Easter is Pentecost. It was the second major celebration of the early church and marks the beginning of the Christian church (Acts 2). It celebrates the coming of the Holy Spirit to the followers of Jesus and marks the fulfillment of his promise to be present with them always. The Sundays following Pentecost are identified by number (Propers) and focuses on the story of the church in mission. On the first Sunday after November 1, the church traditionally celebrates the saints of the church. The last Sunday of Pentecost is Christ the Sovereign Sunday (or Reign of Christ) and marks the anticipation of Christ's return in glory.

What We Bring to Worship

I always bring me
sometimes happy, sometimes sad
sometimes rushed, sometimes bored
sometimes despairing, sometimes hopeful
sometimes anxious, sometimes content
I always bring me

You always bring you
sometimes confident, sometimes scared
sometimes silly, sometimes serious
sometimes guilty, sometimes forgiven
sometimes open, sometimes closed
You always bring you

I always bring me, you always bring you
the real me, the real you
wonderful
imperfect
warm
callous
broken
whole
worthy
unworthy
the real me, the real you
I always bring me, you always bring you

And together we
hear the Word
speak words of faith
eat the Bread
drink from the Cup
confess our sins
hear assuring words
pray for others
pray for ourselves
give thanks to God
are thankful for each other

What we bring is made new
when I bring me, the real me
you bring you, the real you
when we bring ourselves
with each other before God
in worship
and
give what we bring to God
who makes it new[4]

Prayer

Creator God, help me to bring my whole self to worship, so that together with my sisters and brothers in Christ we will be made new. Amen.

Your Thoughts

_____

_____

_____

_____

_____

_____

_____

_____

_____

_____

_____

_____

_____

_____

_____

1.   *Webster's Ninth New Collegiate Dictionary* (Springfield, Mass: Merriam-Webster, 1983).
2.   Ibid.
3.   *United Church of Christ Book of Worship* (New York: United Church of Christ Office for Church Life and Leadership, 1986), 20–24.
4.   "In This Hour," Bulletin Inserts (New York: Office for Church Life and Leadership, 1986). Used by permission.

GOD'S MISSION AND THE

HISTORY OF OUR LOCAL CHURCH

3

Themes

@ Our local church has a history.

@ Our local church has a mission.

@ God's mission and our history connect us to the whole Christian church.

Scriptures

ACTS 11:19–26—The first Christian church in Antioch was started.

MATTHEW 22:34–40—Jesus names the two greatest commandments.

LUKE 4:16–21—Jesus reads from the scroll of Isaiah.

ACTS 2:43–47—Life in the first church in Jerusalem is described.

Before You Gather

Your church has a history and a mission. The history and mission of your church connect it with the whole Christian church. Members of a church are part of a wider Christian community called the Christian church. All have a common beginning in Jesus and the early Christian church. Your church has its own stories to tell of why and how it began. By getting in touch with your church's history and mission, you discover links with its past and reasons for being here and now. It is interesting to learn about the origins and the missionary vision of local churches. Learning about their histories and reasons for being helps to connect the local churches to God's mission and the whole Christian church.

The story in Acts 11:19–26 tells how the first church in Antioch began. Although this wasn't the first church to form after Jesus' resurrection, it was one of the first churches started among people who were not Jews. It was in Antioch that the disciples were first called "Christians" (Acts 11:26).

The other scriptures for this session describe how we are to respond in mission as Christians. Matthew 22:34–40 calls us to love God with all our heart, soul, and mind and our neighbor as ourselves. In Luke 4:18–21, Jesus reads the words from the scroll of Isaiah that describe the call he has come to fulfill. Acts 2:43–47 tells how people in the early church shared their possessions.

In this session, you will take time to explore God's mission and the history of your local church. Each congregation has a story waiting to be told. What gems of history will you find? What things bind you together with the wider church? What things make your local church unique?

There are many dynamics that come into play when a group of people gather to explore God's mission as expressed in the local church. Our understanding of Scripture and what God is trying to say to us helps to shape our response to mission. People bring their experiences and their history in other congregations to the group. Leadership and individual personalities help influence the process. In the end, mission comes about when the Holy Spirit uses the gifts of the members to express God's love to the world.

Questions to Consider

@   What is the mission of your church?

_____

_____

@   How is God using your church to serve the members, the community, and the
    world?

_____

_____

@   How are you a part of the church and its mission?

_____

_____

One Church's Mission Statement

The purpose of our church is

@   to make Christ and the gospel known in the world;

@   to provide opportunities for fellowship; for sharing in experiences of worship,
    renewal, and refreshment; for learning to cope with the problems of life; and for
    understanding the faith;

@   to be a force in the community helping to establish a more Christian social order;

@   to be aware of the needs of our members and the community and to serve those
    needs with concern.[1]

United Church of Christ Statement of Mission[2]

As people of the United Church of Christ, affirming our Statement of Faith, we seek
with the Church Universal to participate in God's mission and to follow the way of
the crucified and risen Christ.

Empowered by the Holy Spirit, we are called and commit ourselves

- to praise God, confess our sin, and joyfully accept God's forgiveness;
- to proclaim the Gospel of Jesus Christ in our suffering world;
- to embody God's love for all people;
- to hear and give voice to creation's cry for justice and peace;
- to name and confront the powers of evil within and among us;
- to repent our silence and complicity with the forces of chaos and death;
- to preach and teach with the power of the Living Word;
- to join oppressed and troubled people in the struggle for liberation;
- to work for justice, healing, and wholeness of life;
- to embrace the unity of Christ's church;
- to discern and celebrate the present and coming reign of God.

Prayer

Holy God, thank you for the church and all those who worship, learn, and grow there. Help us to know that we have a special mission. I pray for your help as I explore what it means to be a faithful member. Amen.

Your Thoughts

_____

_____

_____

_____

_____

_____

_____

_____

_____

_____

_____

_____

_____

_____

_____

_____

_____

_____

_____

_____

1.   "Developing A Mission Statement," in *The Ministry of Volunteers: A Guidebook for Churches* (New York: Office for Church Life and Leadership, 1979).
2.   "United Church of Christ Statement of Mission," Report of General Synod XVI. Used by permission.

The story of the Christian church tells us about how God works in human history.

faith

OUR HISTORY AND HERITAGE

THE BIBLE

4

Themes

- The Bible is a collection of stories that tell us of God's actions toward people and creation—creating, loving, judging, and saving.
- The Bible tells the story of humankind's experience of God.

Scriptures

PSALM 119:97–106—God's word in Scripture is like honey, sweet to the taste; God's word in Scripture is like a lamp that provides light for our way.

2 TIMOTHY 3:14–17—Paul instructs Timothy to trust Scripture as inspired by God.

Before You Gather

Stories are important to our lives. We tell stories to one another almost every day—what happened in school, at a friend's, on vacation. We like to hear stories about what we were like when we were younger, how we learned new skills or showed courage or determination. Even our dreams are stories. Recounting the things that happen to us and to the people around us can help us understand who we are together and where we are going. For the faith community, the Bible is our book of stories. It can help us understand who we are as God's people and what God is calling us to do.

You might wonder how stories from so long ago, spanning several thousand years, about people whose way of life was very different from our own, could be so important for us today. The reason is that the Bible is made up of stories that tell how God's actions—creating, loving, judging, and saving—shaped the lives of the people then and continue to help us today. The Bible is a book that speaks to people of every age and time. By it we are guided, inspired, challenged, and called to be God's co-creators, to love and care for one another and creation. God speaks to us in the Bible through the stories of ordinary people—people who felt the feelings we feel, jealousy, anger, confusion, fear, joy, loneliness, awe. When we listen with open hearts and minds to the stories it contains, the Bible can be a powerful resource in our lives for hope and transformation.

How the Bible Came to Be

Use the following list to fill in the blank and discover how the Bible came to be.

LIST OF WORDS TO FILL IN THE BLANKS

400 C.E.	one thousand	"little books"
1952	people	meditation
Jesus	papyrus	American Standard Version
Greek	Septuagint	Apocrypha
canon	Episcopal	relationship
Thessalonians	oral tradition	Mark
sacred	Latin	storytelling
Vulgate	Reformation	covenant
Paul	King James Version	Acts of the Apostles
sixty-six	English	New Revised Standard Version

The Bible is not just one book but is a collection of _____ books that tell the story of God's _____ with humankind and creation. The word *Bible* comes from *biblia*, a Greek word that means _____. In them the relationship between God and people is communicated through _____—the promises God made with humankind to love, care for, and guide us in the way that gives life. In the Hebrew Scriptures (also known as the Old Testament) the covenant is expressed most simply when God said, "I will walk among you, and I will be your God and you shall be my _____" (Leviticus 26:12). The covenant was also expressed by _____ in the early Christian Scriptures (also known as the New Testament) when he made this promise to the disciples at the Last Supper: "This cup is the new covenant in my blood" (1 Corinthians 11:25b).

The Bible has a rich history of how it came to be. At first, over three thousand years ago, the Hebrews, who were nomads, passed on the stories of God's mighty acts through _____. Many generations learned the stories through this oral tradition. Then, around 1100 B.C.E., the stories were written down in Hebrew, first on stone tablets, then on animal skins and _____. Over time some of the writings took on great importance in the life of the people, and they began to be recognized as special or _____. Around 400 B.C.E. the Jewish people (Hebrews), began the task of deciding which of the writings should be considered sacred and authoritative. These would be called the _____. The books that were included in the Hebrew canon were books of law, history, poetry, and prophets.

Several generations later, in about 285 B.C.E., as the Jewish people settled in different areas and fewer were able to read Hebrew, the Bible was translated into _____. This version was called the _____.

In 98 C.E., some Jewish scholars decided that there were seven books of the Septuagint (SEP–TOO´–A–JINT)—the Greek translation of the Hebrew Bible—written in the three hundred years between the Hebrew Scriptures and the early

Christian Scriptures, that should no longer be a part of the canon. These books,

known as the _____, are available in some translations of the

Bible. The _____ and Roman Catholic Churches consider them as

official and use them in worship and education. Other Christians sometimes use

them for personal reflection and _____.

The earliest Christian Scriptures were the letters that _____ wrote

to various churches and people, the earliest being the letter to the

_____, in about 50 C.E. The Gospels were written down much

later, and came from the _____ of faithful people telling the stories

for several generations. The first gospel to be written was _____,

around 70 C.E. The Gospel of Matthew was written around 85 C.E., as was the

Gospel of Luke. The Gospel of John was the last one to be written down, sometime

around 100 C.E. The writer who wrote Luke also wrote the book of the

_____. Greek was the language in which the Gospels were written.

The canon for the early Christian Scriptures was decided about _____

after years of discussion and disagreement about which books should be

considered sacred and authoritative. Then, around 500 C.E., an official version of

the Bible was translated into _____. It was known as the Latin

_____ (meaning "to make common").

After the_____, in the 1500s, the Bible was made available to the

people in many languages, since most people did not read Latin. Around 1530

William Tyndale translated the Bible into _____ from the

Hebrew and Greek versions. In 1611, the _____ was printed.

The _____ was printed almost three hundred years later. In

_____, the Revised Standard Version was published. Most

recently, the _____ was printed in 1989. Today the Bible has

been translated into more than _____ languages.

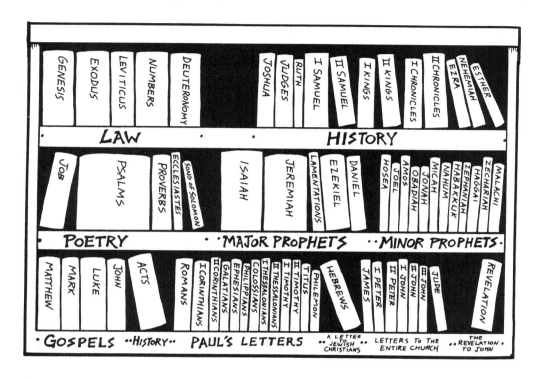

GENESIS · EXODUS · LEVITICUS · NUMBERS · DEUTERONOMY · JOSHUA · JUDGES · RUTH · I SAMUEL · II SAMUEL · I KINGS · II KINGS · I CHRONICLES · II CHRONICLES · EZRA · NEHEMIAH · ESTHER

LAW · · · HISTORY

JOB · PSALMS · PROVERBS · ECCLESIASTES · SONG OF SOLOMON · ISAIAH · JEREMIAH · LAMENTATIONS · EZEKIEL · DANIEL · HOSEA · JOEL · AMOS · OBADIAH · JONAH · MICAH · NAHUM · HABAKKUK · ZEPHANIAH · HAGGAI · ZECHARIAH · MALACHI

· POETRY · · · MAJOR PROPHETS · · · MINOR PROPHETS ·

MATTHEW · MARK · LUKE · JOHN · ACTS · ROMANS · I CORINTHIANS · II CORINTHIANS · GALATIANS · EPHESIANS · PHILIPPIANS · COLOSSIANS · I THESSALONIANS · II THESSALONIANS · I TIMOTHY · II TIMOTHY · TITUS · PHILEMON · HEBREWS · JAMES · I PETER · II PETER · I JOHN · II JOHN · III JOHN · JUDE · REVELATION

· GOSPELS · · HISTORY · · PAUL'S LETTERS · · A LETTER TO JEWISH CHRISTIANS · · LETTERS TO THE ENTIRE CHURCH · · THE REVELATION TO JOHN

What Do We Expect from the Bible?

It is strange that the Bible is our most treasured book, and yet it seems so difficult that we don't find it very helpful. Perhaps we have expected the wrong things of it; we have asked of it what it cannot do. We have expected the Bible to keep promises that it has never made to us. The Bible cannot be a good luck piece to bring God's blessing. Nor can it be an answer book to solve our problems or to give us right belief. So the first question about reading the Bible is what can we indeed expect of it.[1]

—Walter Brueggemann

@   What do you expect from the Bible? Write your thoughts here.

_____

_____

_____

_____

_____

_____

_____

_____

_____

_____

_____

_____

_____

_____

How to Read the Bible

How *do* you read the Bible? Here are some suggestions:

@ Begin with prayer. Ask the Holy Spirit to open your heart and mind as you read and reflect on the Bible verses.

@ Read the verses out loud. Notice words that stir some feelings in you—curiosity, fear, doubt, peace, challenge, hope. Write down the words if you want. Write down the questions or insights that come to you as you read.

@ Think about the one who first wrote the words. Who was it? What was it like in the world at that time? Why did the writer write these words? What problem or situation is being addressed? A good Bible commentary or Bible dictionary can help you answer these questions.

@ Think about the people the message was for. Who were the first hearers of this story? What did the passage mean to them? What difference could it have made in their lives?

@ Write down your thoughts and discoveries in your journal or notebook. Use Bible study tools such as atlases, concordances, Bible dictionaries, and commentaries to help you find the answers to questions you still have. Other church members can help too.

@ When you have taken these steps, then ask yourself:

What have I learned about God from this passage?

What have I learned about myself from this passage?

What have I learned about others from this passage?

If I take this passage to heart, how am I being asked to change or grow?

How is my faith community being asked to change or grow?

In what ways do I feel helped or healed by this passage?

How does the passage help my faith community?

Prayer

Help your Word come alive within me, O God, as I discover the power of the stories in the Bible. Amen.

Your Thoughts

_____

_____

_____

_____

_____

_____

_____

_____

_____

_____

_____

_____

_____

_____

_____

_____

_____

_____

_____

_____

1.   Walter Brueggemann, *The Bible Makes Sense* (Winona, Minn.: St. Mary's Press, 1977), 9.

THE HISTORY OF CHRISTIANITY

Themes

@ The Christian church was called into being by the life, witness, death, and resurrection of Jesus Christ.

@ The story of the Christian church tells us about how God works in human history.

@ The Christian church is more than a human organization, it is a gift from God.

Scriptures

MATTHEW 16:13–20—Jesus affirms Peter's faith as a foundation for understanding God's call.

EPHESIANS 11:11–22—Jesus Christ is the cornerstone of our faith.

HEBREWS 12:1–2—Many faithful people, led by Jesus' example, have gone before us and encourage our faith.

Before You Gather

"Who do you say that I am?" That question, asked by Jesus of Simon Peter, opened the door for Peter to declare without question who Jesus was. Peter's response was simple, only ten words—"You are the Messiah, the Child of the living God" (Matthew 16:16). He answered quickly—stating what was obvious to him. But Jesus' reaction to these ten words was to say, "Your name is

Peter [meaning rock], and on this rock I will build my church."

The Christian church is built on the rock of Peter's faith. What it has in common, over the ages and generations, is that those who call themselves Christian do so because they simply *know who Jesus is*. The disciples came to know Jesus as Messiah from their personal contact with him, and from the impact he had on their lives. In the early years of Christianity, those who had built their faith on "Christ Jesus . . . as the cornerstone" (Ephesians 2:20) did so at great risk. They could have been persecuted or put to death. Later Christians watched as their faith became merged with society; and in the Middle Ages, the flickering light of learning was kept alive through the efforts of Christians who thought it important to maintain the books that recorded the events of their faith. But for Christians across all the ages, bound together by the simple fact of knowing who Jesus was, their connection with those who went before (the "cloud of witnesses" of Hebrews 12:1) helped them think of themselves as a special people. "So then you are no longer strangers and aliens, but you are citizens with the saints and also members of the household of God, built upon the foundation of the apostles and prophets, with Christ Jesus himself as the cornerstone . . . you also are built together spiritually into a dwelling place for God" (Ephesians 2:19–22).

In a very real way, confirmation is about helping persons and communities to become a dwelling place for God. We are invited to join centuries upon centuries of believers who have been willing to do what Peter did, to say aloud who Jesus is. That dwelling place for God in us is built upon a foundation of prophets and apostles, upon stories of the faithful, upon the efforts of a cloud of witnesses to share what is real. Hearing their words gives us confidence to say them for ourselves: "You are the Messiah, the Child of the living God."

A Walk through Church History: Create a Time Line

A complete survey of the Christian church is far beyond the scope and time limits of this session. Here is a condensed version, beginning with the birth of Jesus and covering the next thousand years of church history. In some cases the years of events are approximate.

THE BEGINNING: THE SEED IS PLANTED (6 B.C.E. TO 30 C.E.)

@ **Jesus is born** when Caesar Augustus is Roman emperor and Herod the Great is king, about 6 B.C.E.

@ After being baptized by John, **Jesus begins his public ministry** of teaching and healing around 26 C.E.; crowds follow him and are amazed, but some reject his message.

@ About 30 C.E., **Jesus** foretells his death, enters Jerusalem, the center of religious and political power, **is arrested, tried, convicted, put to death** on a cross, and laid in a stone tomb; after three days in the tomb **Jesus rises from the dead.**

@ Forty days after his death, **Christ's ascension** occurs, and his physical presence on earth is ended.

@ Fifty days after the resurrection, as Jesus' followers are gathered in a room in Jerusalem to observe the Jewish holy day of Pentecost, the Holy Spirit comes upon the disciples and fills them with inspiration, courage, and power. We call this day **Pentecost, the birthday of the church.**

THE FIRST CHURCH: THE SEED SPROUTS (30 C.E. TO 70 C.E.)

@ **Christ's followers begin to live in community, share possessions, worship together, preach and heal** in the streets after 30 C.E. This history of the early church is recorded later in the book of the Bible called the Acts of the Apostles.

@ In the year 35 C.E., a follower named **Stephen is stoned to death for his belief in Jesus Christ. Persecution of Christians begins.** It will continue, occasionally cruel and severe, for the next 277 years.

@ In the year 40 C.E., a Jewish Roman citizen named Saul, one of the great persecutors of Christians, is going to a meeting in Damascus to plan future persecutions. On the road to Damascus **Saul has a vision of Christ, becomes a believer, and changes his name to Paul.**

@ About 47 C.E. **Paul begins his first missionary tour** to the Gentiles (non-Jews), preaching and starting new churches.

@ As Paul begins his work a problem arises for the young church. Up to this point, new Christians had come from the Jewish tradition, but through Paul's ministries Gentiles (non-Jews) are becoming Christians. In 49 C.E. **a council is held in Jerusalem** between Paul and the other apostles. A decision is made, with the guidance of the Holy Spirit, that **the Good News of Jesus Christ is for all people.** Peter and the other apostles will work and build the church among the Jews, while Paul and his co-workers will work among the Gentiles.

@ From 47 to 64 C.E., **Paul and others**, such as Silas, Timothy, Barnabas, Priscilla, Aquilla, **start and support new churches.**

@ **Paul writes letters to these new churches.** These are the first Christian writings that we know of. Many of these letters are found in the New Testament.

@ In 64 C.E. the Roman government begins persecuting Christians; both **Paul and Peter are martyred** because of their faith.

THE NEXT GENERATION: THE FIRST STEM (70 C.E. TO 300 C.E.)

@ In the years 70 to 90 C.E. **the church spreads rapidly.** Church leaders realize Christ's promised return will not happen soon. To help teach about Christ, and to keep the story from being altered, **accounts of Jesus' life are recorded** in Greek, the common language of the day. As many as twelve of these accounts, known as **Gospels,** are written. Four of the best and most reliable accounts are distributed widely. They are Matthew, Mark, Luke, and John.

@ Around 100 C.E. **the Pastoral Epistles are written.** They deal with theological and church issues as the church grows and becomes more organized.

@ By the year 135 C.E. church leaders gather all the trustworthy Christian writings (Pauline letters, Gospels, and Epistles), compile them into one book, and decree that these writings are the "canon," which means "measuring rod or rule for faith." They are considered holy and cannot be changed. **The New Testament is completed.**

@ During the years 185 to 235 C.E. there is phenomenal **growth of Christianity in African, Mediterranean, and Middle Eastern** regions. Centers of faith arise in Carthage and Alexandria in northern Africa and in Rome. Persecution approaching the year 300 becomes particularly brutal.

A NEW ERA: THE STEM BEGINS TO BRANCH OUT (300 C.E. TO 1000 C.E.)

@ In 312 C.E., after winning the battle of Milvan Bridge, **Constantine** becomes the emperor of the Roman Empire and **makes Christianity a legalized religion.** For the first time it is lawful to be a Christian in the Roman Empire.

@ Church leaders gather and meet in councils to discuss church problems, administration, and theological issues. Over the years, the identity of Jesus has been misinterpreted, distorted, and confused with ideas from non-Christian philosophies. In 325 C.E., at the Council of Nicea, church officials further clarify their understanding of who Jesus was and offer a guideline for what Christians believe. **The Nicene Creed is written.**

@ In disagreement with a decision made at the **Council of Chalcedon** in 451 C.E., one group representing churches in Africa separates to form the Coptic Church.

@ In 520 C.E. a Christian named **Benedict begins a reform movement** in the church. He gathers a group to live a secluded, simple life of service, seeking religious purity rather than wealth or power. They are the first monks. This monastic order immediately grows in popularity.

@ Around 600 C.E. **the Roman church sends missionaries to Northern Europe**—Boniface to Germanic peoples and Patrick to Irish peoples. In 862 C.E. the brothers Cyril and Methodious leave Constantinople to go to Moravia. They are known as the apostles to the Slavs.

@ In 800 C.E. in what is now France, **Charlemagne becomes the Roman emperor.** He champions Christianity and gives his subjects two choices—baptism or death. **The Western church grows.**

THE CHURCH IN POWER: THE TREE FORMS TWO MAIN BRANCHES (1000 C.E. TO 1500 C.E.)

@ Due largely to disagreements with decisions made and enforced by the powerful Roman church, the Eastern church, centered in Constantinople, separates from the Western church. In 1054 C.E. an event known as the **Great Schism happens.** The Eastern Orthodox church and the Western Roman church are formally split.

@ During the years 1096 to 1272 C.E. the Western church sends crusaders to invade and recapture the Holy Land for Christianity by driving out the Muslims. In this troubling time in history the church becomes an instrument of violence, genocide, and colonial aggression. **The Crusades** fail at their goal, but economic trade between the East and West is established.

@ From 1100 to 1500 C.E. **the Roman church grows in wealth and power,** leading to corruption. Church positions, such as bishop, are sold to the highest bidder. Sins are forgiven if a fee, called an indulgence, is paid to the church. In addition to the corruption, only priests are allowed to read scripture, receive Holy Communion, or sing hymns. Though churches serve people in areas of different cultures and languages, people are forced to worship and hear the Bible read only in Latin. Protests arise, but attempted reforms are always crushed by the powerful church authorities.

ℰ From 1300 to 1550 C.E. many heroic protestors who confront the corruption and stand up to the church leadership are killed. **John Huss is burnt at the stake** in 1415. **Joan of Arc is killed** in 1431.

ℰ The "Latin-only" barrier for the reading of Scripture is eventually broken in 1382, when **John Wycliffe translates the Bible into English.** In 1450, the movable type printing press is invented and mass production of Bibles becomes possible. Now people may own and read their own Bibles.

THE REFORMATION: NEW BRANCHES SPROUT (1500 C.E. TO 1600 C.E.)

ℰ With corruption continuing in the Roman church and its leaders unwilling to change, many brave critics continue to speak out. In 1517 a priest named **Martin Luther nails 95 theses (statements) on the door of the parish church in Wittenburg, Germany,** suggesting the reforms the church must make. He has no intention of breaking away or starting a new church, only of reforming the Roman church. The church leaders refuse to discuss his reforms and force him publicly to recant his criticism of the church. Luther refuses, saying: "Here I stand, I cannot do otherwise." With the backing of the German prince, he leaves the Roman church and forms the Luthern Church. **The Reformation of the church begins.** Luther translates the Bible into German and reintroduces congregational singing, writing hymns of his own.

ℰ In Switzerland in 1525, **Ulrich Zwingli makes more reforms.** His attempt to greatly simplify the church results in **the formation of the Reformed Church.** Other reformers called Anabaptists reject all forms of church government in reaction to the domination by the Roman church leadership.

- In 1534 the Reformation continues in England when **Henry VIII** splits with Rome and **creates the Church of England (Anglican),** governed and administered by English Parliament.

- In 1550, another reformer in Switzerland, **John Calvin, creates the Presbyterian Church,** which has a new style of church government—a church led by a panel of presbyters. Calvin seeks to transform Geneva into a model city of Christian life.

THE REFORM CONTINUES: MORE BRANCHES (1600 C.E. TO 1700 C.E.)

- From 1545 to 1563 **the Roman Catholic Church reforms** with the Council of Trent. In the meantime, many of the Reformation Churches have become just as dictatorial, oppressive, and laden with church hierarchy and government as before.

- In England, just before 1600, many revolt against strict Anglican rules and government interference. This group separates to form their own groups. John Bunyan wrote A *Pilgrim's Progress* to urge these oppressed Christians to keep the faith. In 1581 **a congregation formed** by Robert Browne came to be **called "Brownists" or "Separatists."**

- In 1604 another small group chooses to separate from the English establishment church. These Separatists form their own congregation and move to Holland for religious freedom. These Separatists, called **Pilgrims,** cross the Atlantic Ocean. In 1620 they **land at Plymouth Rock** in what is now Massachusetts. In 1629 they are joined by a group of **Puritans** who **arrive from England.**

- In 1648, at a conference of Puritans and Pilgrims, **the Cambridge Platform is produced.** This document deals with questions about the order and organization of Congregational Churches in America. These congregations are the forerunners of the United Church of Christ.

A UNIQUE CHURCH IS FORMED: THE TREE BEARS FRUIT
(1700 C.E. TO PRESENT)

- In 1710, with depression and hard times in Europe, groups of **German and Swiss immigrants settle in North America** in the middle Atlantic states. Having come from areas of Europe where the Reformed Church was popular, these immigrants gather **and form** here what will also later become known as **the Reformed Church.**

- In 1738, **John Wesley**, a leader in the Church of England, feels his "heart strangely warmed" as the words of Martin Luther are read. The next year he **organizes the first Methodist congregation.**

- In 1820 in the United States of America, Methodists under **James O'Kelly,** Presbyterians under **Barton Stone,** and Baptists under **Abner Jones form** a loose association of churches, which become **the Christian Church.** It is a predecessor to the United Church of Christ.

- In 1832 this Christian Church is torn apart over conflicts surrounding baptism and Holy Communion. Over time, some split to **form the Churches of Christ, Disciples of Christ, and the Christian Churches.**

- In 1840 **German immigrants** who had settled in the Mississippi Valley, finding a common bond in their faith, **form the Evangelical Synod** in Missouri.

- In 1853 **Antoinette Brown Blackwell is ordained** into Christian ministry. She is the first woman ordained as a Congregational minister.

- In 1931 **the Congregational and Christian Churches merge to form the Congregational Christian Churches.**

- Three years later, in 1934, **the Reformed Church and the Evangelical Synod merge to form the Evangelical and Reformed Church.**

- These two denominations, the Congregational Christian and Evangelical and Reformed, have much in common. They both emphasize a strong personal faith as

well as a strong social responsibility to care for the powerless and to bring justice
to the oppressed. They both take seriously Jesus' prayer "that all may be one," as
recorded in John. These two denominations believe in Christian unity and the
importance of working with other denominations. In 1957, after much discussion,
prayer, and guidance by the Holy Spirit, the United Church of Christ is formed
through the merger of the Congregational Christian Churches and the Evangelical
and Reformed Church. The new denomination's government (polity) is based neither on the episcopal system (with bishops and hierarchy) or the presbyterian system (with a board of presbyters who decide for their congregations). **The United
Church of Christ adopts a covenantal polity** that affirms the autonomy of
each local church to make its own decisions in faith, while remaining connected
and accountable to other local churches through associations. The denomination is
comprised of three interrelated groups: local churches, conferences, and the
national body of instrumentalities and agencies. These bodies work in partnership
with the others.

@   After 1957, the tree of Christianity continues to change. **The Roman Catholic
Church experiences a reform movement called Vatican II** in 1964. **The
Evangelical United Brethren merge with the Methodist Church to
form the United Methodist Church** in 1968. The northern and southern
Presbyterian churches unite to form the Presbyterian Church U.S.A. in 1983.
The **Lutheran Churches join to become the Evangelical Lutheran
Church in America** in 1986. The reformation of Christianity continues.

Prayer

Gracious and loving God, thank you for the gift of the church—a community of people around the world who follow Christ and live in hope. Help me to learn from the faithful people of yesterday and those who are following Christ today. Amen.

Your Thoughts

_____

_____

_____

_____

_____

_____

_____

_____

_____

_____

_____

_____

_____

_____

_____

_____

_____

_____

_____

THE HISTORY OF THE

UNITED CHURCH OF CHRIST

Themes

- The United Church of Christ is a uniting church.
- The United Church of Christ is an expression of the universal Christian church.
- The United Church of Christ is organized into settings for ministry and mission.

Scriptures

JOHN 17:20–23—Jesus prays that his followers may all be one.

1 CORINTHIANS 12:4–11—There are a variety of spiritual gifts in the church.

EPHESIANS 4:4–6, 11–16—There is Christian unity amid the diversity of gifts.

Before You Gather

Look at our name—the United Church of Christ! Our motto is: "That they all may be one." One is an important word in the Bible. In the gospels of Matthew and John alone, this word is used nearly three hundred times. When Jesus prayed to God for his followers, he asked "that they may be one, as we are one" (John 17:21). For Jesus, unity was an important idea.

Uniting people has been part of God's plan all along. Jesus' prayer, the one he prayed before he was arrested and condemned to death, is called the "high priestly prayer" and is found in John 17. It helps us to understand that unity is a result of God's action toward us and does not come from our efforts alone. It also lets us know that when we strive for unity with others, the world is made better.

Since there is much diversity among those who follow Christ, we might ask, "What does 'being one' mean for us in this day? Do we all need to be a part of the same organization or denomination to show unity? Do we all need to believe exactly the same things and have the same understanding of mission? Are the various Christian denominations a sign of disunity, weakness, and brokenness which someday may be 'overcome'? Or, are denominations a way to be united in Christ even though we are diverse and different?"

The United Church of Christ tries to bring about church unity both by working together with other denominations *and* by honoring the distinctions among the worldwide Christian community. There are many stories that support this inclusiveness in our history. African Americans, Armenians, Asians, European Americans, Hispanics, native Hawaiians, Hungarians, Native Americans, Samoans, and many others have shaped the denomination. Our denomination is the result of a merger in 1957 of two distinct bodies: the Evangelical and Reformed Church and the Congregational Christian Churches. The Evangelical and Reformed Church was a result of a 1934 merger of the Reformed Church in the United States and the Evangelical Synod of North America. The Congregational Christian Churches were formed in 1931, bringing together the General Convention of the South, which included the African American Convention, and the National Council of the Congregational Churches. Since the time of the merger the United Church of Christ has been in conversation with other Christian churches around issues of unity through the Consultation on Church Union (COCU). Also, the United Church of Christ is joined in a partnership with the Christian Church (Disciples of Christ) in the Common Global Ministries Board, which coordinates a program of common mission ministries around the world through the United Church Board for World Ministries (UCC) and the Division of Overseas Ministries (CC(DoC)). The United Church of Christ also participates in interchurch bodies such as the National Council of Churches, the World Council of Churches, and the World Alliance of Reformed Churches.

We are the *United* Church of Christ. Working for unity yet celebrating diversity is, at times, a difficult balancing act. Paul speaks to this in his letter to the Corinthians, pointing out that while Christians have been given different gifts, "to each is given the manifestation of the Spirit for the common good" (1 Corinthians 12:7). In the letter to the Ephesians, Paul affirms that there is "one Sovereign, one faith, one baptism, one God of all" (4:5–6). Paul made this claim during the first century after Christ, when the church was already divided into many different factions. His message is just as important now as it was then: the church, though divided into many denominations and communities, is still one in Christ.

In the same way, our forebears in the United Church of Christ were concerned with both a *personal faith* as guided by the Holy Spirit and the Scriptures and the *social responsibility* of continuing Jesus' ministry of healing, feeding, comforting, and freeing. While ultimate authority is lodged in Christ as the head of the church, we rely on the inspired and informed word of individual members, local churches, associations, conferences, the General Synod, and national offices and instrumentalities working in covenantal partnership to carry out the ministry and mission of Jesus Christ. See the chart on page 68 which outlines the relationships and functions of the United Church of Christ.

The church in all that it does must continually be renewed by the power of the Holy Spirit to meet changing times. What the church has been in its history is important and valuable, but what the church will yet become is just as important and valuable. You are an important part of this future!

Questions to Consider

- Where did this denomination begin?

- What was happening in history when this church began?

- What were its main beliefs?

- What special mission focus did it have?

- What beliefs form the basis for the United Church of Christ?

- Looking at the history of the United Church of Christ, how does your local church continue to benefit from the history and heritage of our forebears in faith?

- Looking at the United Church of Christ or your local church, how do you respect the differences of others while at the same time seeking to be united?

- In what ways are we united in spite of our differences?

- How might the United Church of Christ best live out its motto "That they may all be one"?

- What signs are there in the United Church of Christ that it has tried in its history to be inclusive of God's people from a variety of cultures and races?

- Often these histories are hidden stories. Sometimes a preference for one story or point of view hides the fact that others have been involved in the history all along. How can you find a way to tell the rich and varied history of the United Church of Christ?

The Roots of the United Church of Christ[1]

THE CONGREGATIONAL CHURCHES

Many years ago, small groups of Christians in England were trying to live as they believed a true Christian people should live. In 1571 all English people were told by the government that they should belong to the Anglican Church. It would be the state church and it would be ruled by leaders appointed by the ruler of England.

Some of the Christians did not believe that they could belong to the state church. They did not think it was true to Jesus' teachings. These people joined together and called themselves Separatists.

The leaders of the state church began to harass the Separatist leaders. They even put some in prison. Some of the Separatists left England and went to Holland to find freedom to worship and believe as they wanted. But Holland was strange to them and they didn't want their children to become Dutch citizens. They were English. They wanted to bring their children up to follow their customs and to speak the English language.

So, in 1620 over one hundred persons boarded a ship called the *Mayflower* and set out for the New World. These colonists, who later were called Pilgrims, landed at Plymouth Rock in what is now Massachusetts. They came to Plymouth in the hope of building "a city on a hill," an idea based on the images in the book of Revelation of a holy city devoted to God (Revelation 21) and outlined in the Mayflower Compact.

It was a struggle for them to adjust to the new country. Another group—called Puritans because they wished to purify the church—formed the Massachusetts Bay Colony. Soon the Pilgrims and the Puritans joined together for mutual support. The Cambridge Platform of 1648 stated their beliefs and became the basis for Congregationalism: Christ is the sole head of the church; the visible church is a particular congregation; and the church is composed of regenerate and holy believers gathered in covenant together to preserve communion with each other for the sake of unity in Christ.[2] They established churches and other community groups. By 1640 there were thirty-five churches, and they now were called Congregationalists. Their leaders—John Winthrop, John Endicott, Frances Higginson, and Samuel Skelton—helped each church write its own covenant (agreement) about their relationships with one another and with God. They insisted that each local church make its own decisions so that they would be free.

THE CHRISTIAN CHURCHES

In search of religious freedom and liberty, three groups of new colonists formed
churches during the late 1790s and early 1800s. Each group was determined to
avoid any name except the one that each found best suited: Christian. One
group began in North Carolina, another in Kentucky, and a third in Vermont.

James O'Kelly was the central figure in the North Carolina movement. He was a
Christian with deep convictions. He led others to stand up for their beliefs. He
believed that the Bible alone could guide faith and its practice. He believed
that Christian character was the only requirement for Christian fellowship and
church membership, and he taught that Jesus was the only head of the church.

Elias Smith, Abner Jones, and Barton Stone were leaders of the other groups who
also called themselves Christians. These groups believed that the followers of
Christ did not need a large organization with many rules. Their purpose was to
reform the world and to bring all Christians together.

In 1808 these groups published the first religious newspaper in the United States.
They started colleges for women and men. They wanted educated ministers
and lay persons too. They insisted on equal numbers of lay and ministerial
leaders in their local and conference organizations.

In 1810 the three groups agreed to join together in their mission: to unite the followers of Jesus Christ that the world might believe. They were truly pioneers
for Christ.

In 1931 the Congregational Churches and the Christian Churches joined together
to become the *Congregational Christian Churches*.

THE REFORMED CHURCH IN THE UNITED STATES

The Reformed Church began in Switzerland and Germany in the sixteenth century. The Reformers stressed the necessity of faith as a basis for communion with
Christ.

Economic hardships caused many reformers to leave the Palatine (southwest) area of Germany in the late 1600s and come to this country. Many of these German immigrants settled in Pennsylvania, Maryland, and the Shenandoah Valley of Virginia. No matter where they settled, the German Reformed people organized religious services. Some groups had prayers once a day and two sermons on Sunday. This was the beginning of the German Reformed Church in the United States.

Later on, Reformed immigrants from Switzerland, many of whom settled in Wisconsin, became members. Much later a group of congregations made up of Reformed immigrants from Hungary joined the church, which by this time had dropped the word German in its name.

The first congregations were the work of John Philip Boehm, a Pennsylvania school teacher, who founded a church at Faulkner Swamp in 1725. His friend Michael Schlatter began the formal organization of a synod, which brought the churches together to help one another.

This denomination established many schools, two seminaries to train ministers, several colleges, and a board of foreign missions. It continued to build new churches as well. Some of the West Coast churches included people of Asian background.

THE EVANGELICAL SYNOD OF NORTH AMERICA

In 1817, the Lutheran and the Reformed Churches in Germany united to form the Evangelical Church, first in Prussia and then in the other German states. Unrest among German Christians over the government's control of the church as well as hard times led many of these Germans to come to the United States beginning in the 1830s. They called themselves Evangelical and insisted that Christianity was a practical religion, not just knowledge.

Many of these immigrants settled in Missouri, Illinois, and Indiana, with St. Louis as the center. In 1840 they organized the German Evangelical Church Society of the West (*Die Kirchenverein des Westens*). George Wall, Joseph Rieger, and Adolph Baltzer were influential leaders who helped to organize the immigrants into churches throughout the midwestern states.

Their leaders encouraged members to provide homes for orphans and the aged, hospitals for the sick, and care for the underprivileged. Some of the churches provided their own schools since many communities did not have public schools. Along with their work in these missions, they established a magazine called *Der Friedensbote* (*Messenger of Peace*). After the Civil War, the Church Society joined with other groups to form the Evangelical Synod of North America.

By the early 1900s the Synod began to stress Christian education, evangelism, and social action. It also sent missionaries to other lands. Because the Evangelical Church in Germany had been formed by a union of Lutheran and Reformed groups, the Evangelical Synod worked well with other denominations in interchurch projects.

In 1934 the Reformed Church in the United States and the Evangelical Synod of North America joined together to form the *Evangelical and Reformed Church.*

Diversity in the United Church of Christ

The United Church of Christ is united by more than the merger of two denominations; it is united by the stories of many people. Here are some examples:

℮ The first Armenian church established in North America was the Armenian Congregational Church of the Martyrs in Worcester, Massachusetts, in 1881. This church and others that followed were made up of Armenian immigrants who were fleeing the persecution and terrible oppression of the Turkish government of the late 1800s and early 1900s.

- In 1874, the first Japanese American minister, Neesima Jo (Joseph Hardy Neesima), was ordained by the Evangelical Church. He returned to Japan with the support of the predecessor denominations of the United Church of Christ to found Doshisha University, a Christian college in Kyoto.

- Between 1885 and 1926, fifteen Japanese American churches affiliated with the Congregational Church came into being. They were located in California, Utah, and Washington.

- In 1964 both Native American and non–Native American leaders in the United Church of Christ, acknowledging a long and devastating history of racism in the relationship of the church's mission to the Native Americans since the early 1600s, met in Aberdeen, South Dakota. At that consultation they struggled to find a way to bring about "mission with" rather than "mission to" Indian people. In 1970 the Council for American Indian Ministry (of the United Church of Christ) was founded, based on the idea of self-determination and justice for Native Americans.

- The African American history in the United Church of Christ spans many years and reflects the creative and faithful determination of a deeply religious people to express hope in the midst of oppression. In 1852 the Providence Church in Chesapeake, Virginia, was founded by free black Christians. Other churches throughout North Carolina and Virginia were started in the late 1800s. By 1916 there were churches in New Jersey, New York, Alabama, Georgia, Pennsylvania, and mission churches in British Guiana, South America, and Trinidad. In 1950 the Convention of the South of the Congregational Christian Churches was formed under the leadership of J. Taylor Stanley, bringing together black congregations from Virginia to Texas. Many of the churches became a part of the local associations of the United Church of Christ when it was formed and dissolved the Convention of the South. Today a recognized interest group called United Black Christians as well as the Commission for Racial Justice help to keep alive the legacy and traditions of the black church in the United Church of Christ.

@ There is a strong and vibrant ministry of Hispanic churches—numbering more than ninety congregations—in the United Church of Christ. They are located in cities and towns in Puerto Rico, New York, Illinois, Texas, Ohio, Pennsylvania, California, Florida, Massachusetts, Connecticut, and Rhode Island, and many other communities across the country. Hispanic congregations bring to the United Church of Christ a rich worship tradition, a strong need to serve the community, and a desire to eliminate injustice. The Council for Hispanic Ministries of the United Church of Christ, organized in 1977, continues to promote these hopes for the church.

@ The United Church of Christ has valued the gifts and insights of youth and young adults in many ways throughout its history. In the mid-1900s Youth Caravans, groups of youth trained to work as volunteers at various mission sites, traveled the country during the summers to serve, learn, and grow in faith. Today the Volunteer Service Ministry of the United Church of Christ continues to encourage youth and young adult involvement in the life of the church. In 1981 the General Synod, meeting in Rochester, New York, voted to make youth and youth adult concerns a priority of the church. Since then more youth and young adults have had voice and vote on boards, committees, and delegations of the church. This priority continues to be supported by meetings such as the National and Regional Youth Events.

@ In the late 1800s, many Chinese people, escaping drought, war, and famine in China, came to the United States in search of a better life. Many settled in northern California. Living conditions were still difficult and prejudice was widespread. The Congregational Church, through the efforts of the American Missionary Association, founded several schools among the Chinese people. Many of these schools evolved into churches that are active today—in San Francisco, San Diego, and Berkeley. In the 1970s, new Chinese churches were founded in Seattle, Detroit, and the Boston area.

@ In 1974 a group called the Pacific and Asian American Ministries (PAAM) of the United Church of Christ was formed. It includes representatives from the historical

Chinese churches along with Samoan, Hawaiian, Japanese, and other churches with large Asian and Pacific Islander memberships. It gathers for fellowship, support, and advocacy for Asian and Pacific Islanders.

❧ In 1987 the General Synod of the United Church of Christ called upon local churches and other denominational groups to go through a time of study and reflection and consider declaring themselves open and affirming of gay men, lesbians, and bisexuals and to adopt nondiscrimination policies.

❧ The impact of women's leadership in the United Church of Christ and its predecessor denominations is significant. Modeled after the many women who were preachers, teachers, leaders, and healers in the early church—Phoebe, Lydia, Priscilla, and others—women in the United Church of Christ have been leaders in justice ministry, mission work, and outreach. They have been deaconesses, trained to work in hospitals and homes established by the churches, and consecrated for this ministry. They have been missionaries, teachers, and workers dedicated to ending social problems. They have been ordained clergy and lay workers in the church. In 1853 Antoinette Brown Blackwell was ordained by a small Congregational Church in South Butler, New York. She was the first ordained woman in one of the denominations that eventually formed the United Church of Christ. Today there are many women clergy in the United Church of Christ.

The United Church of Christ Is . . . [3]

The United Church of Christ is a *united* and a *uniting* church. Each of the communions which came together to form the United Church of Christ in 1957 had itself come into being through the union of two denominations. Therefore, church union and Christian unity are in the very bloodstream of our people.

The United Church of Christ is a church of *Christ*. We believe that we are called to carry out Christ's mission in the world today. Wherever there are people without the gospel, wherever there are people in need, wherever there is injustice, strife, hatred, and greed—there the Church of Christ is bound by its Sovereign to bear witness, to serve, to help, to reconcile, to rebuild. We belong to *Christ* and we must follow where Christ leads.

The United Church of Christ is a *free* church and a *responsible* church. No one dictates to a local church concerning the decisions it makes. Freedom is guaranteed. But it is "freedom in the gospel" (cf. Galatians 2:4) and assumes that every corporate body within the church, whether a local church or a conference or the General Synod, will make its decisions in the light of the gospel and out of a sense of responsibility to the whole fellowship.

The United Church of Christ is a church *of the people*. The church is not the clergy, not the organization at the regional or national levels, not the officers or boards, commissions or councils, though all play their important and indispensable parts. The church is the *people* gathered for worship, work, and witness. The local and regional mission and the wider mission to the nation and the world through the instrumentalities of the denomination are made possible by the response of persons to the task and witness entrusted to us together as *people* of God.

The Emblem of the United Church of Christ

This emblem is based on the ancient Christian symbol known as the Cross of Victory or the Cross Triumphant. Traditionally, this symbol—the cross grounded in the circle and topped with a crown—tells of the sovereign power of the risen Christ over all the world. The circle, representing the world, is divided into three parts and refers to Christ's command in Acts 1:8 to the disciples: "You will be my witnesses in Jerusalem, and in all Judea and Samaria, and to the ends of the earth." The emblem also includes the United Church of Christ motto: "That they may all be one" (John 17:21).

The Structure of the United Church of Christ

LOCAL CHURCHES

ASSOCIATIONS AND CONFERENCES OF CHURCHES AND MINISTERS

GENERAL SYNOD

(The representative, deliberative body of the United Church of Christ, composed of 675 to 725 church members elected by their conferences. Meets biennially. Offers: Moderator, President, Secretary, and Director of Finance and Treasurer.)

EXECUTIVE COUNCIL

(Acts for General Synod between Synod sessions. Standing committees: Administrative, Finance and Budget, Planning and Correlation, Structural Planning.)

| UNITED CHURCH BOARD FOR HOMELAND MINISTRIES | UNITED CHURCH BOARD FOR WORLD MINISTRIES | UNITED CHURCH PENSION BOARDS | UNITED CHURCH FOUNDATION | OFFICE FOR CHURCH IN SOCIETY | OFFICE FOR CHURCH LIFE AND LEADERSHIP | OFFICE OF COMMUNICATION | STEWARDSHIP COUNCIL |

| Council for Racial and Ethnic Ministries | Commission for Racial Justice | Commission on Development | Coordinating Center for Women in Church and Society | Council for Ecumenism | Historical Council | Council for American Indian Ministries |

This chart is not designed to indicate legal or administrative structure.

Prayer

Holy One, thank you for the courage and faithfulness of those who helped to form the United Church of Christ. Help me to learn from their wisdom and ways to be open to the gifts that each person brings to life. In Christ's name, amen.

Your Thoughts

_____

_____

_____

_____

_____

_____

_____

_____

_____

_____

_____

_____

_____

_____

_____

_____

_____

_____

1. Louis H. Gunnemann, *The Shaping of the United Church of Christ: An Essay in the History of American Christianity* (New York: United Church Press, 1989). Used by permission.
2. Williston Walker, *Creeds and Platforms of Congregationalism* (New York: The Pilgrim Press, 1991), 194–237. Used by permission.
3. Adapted from a statement by Robert V. Moss, president (1969–1976), United Church of Christ , *Confirming Our faith: A Confirmation Resource for the United Church of Christ.* (New York: United Church Press, 1980). Used by permission.

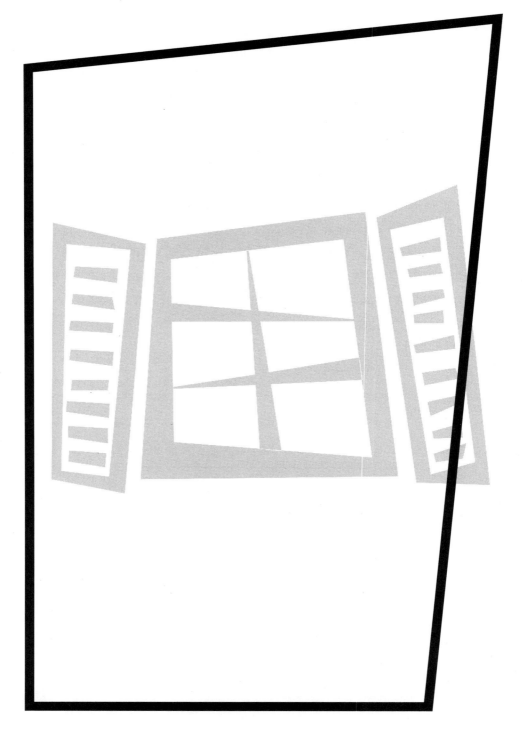

THE STATEMENT OF FAITH

7

Themes

- The United Church of Christ Statement of Faith affirms God's deeds and encourages our faithful response.
- There are many ways to express our faith.

Scriptures

ACTS 10:34–43—Peter tells the good news of Jesus Christ.

JOHN 3:16–21—God's saving love is for the whole world.

ROMANS 12:9–21—Paul provides guidelines for Christian living.

Before You Gather

What does the United Church of Christ have in common with other Christian churches? This question may be just as important as its partner, "What makes the United Church of Christ different?" Both questions help us think about what it means to be a church and about how our faith in Jesus Christ is shown. To be active participants in the church of Jesus Christ, it is important to know who we are and what we believe. A creed can help us with this. A creed is a statement of belief or a confession of faith. In the United Church of Christ we share the common and ancient creeds of the Christian faith—the Apostles'

Creed and the Nicene Creed. But there is another statement, unique to the
United Church of Christ, which unites us as a denomination. It is the
Statement of Faith.

The Statement of Faith, first written in 1959 and rewritten in its more prayerful and
doxological form in 1981, tells the glorious deeds of God. It is not a creed or test
of faith. Rather, it declares the activity of God in Jesus Christ, the Holy Spirit,
and the church, and it outlines the promises made to those who enter a trusting
relationship with God. It originated as a statement of common beliefs written to
celebrate the birth of the United Church of Christ in 1957, uniting the
Congregational Christian Churches and the Evangelical and Reformed Church.

At the large, national meeting (called the General Synod) in Cleveland, Ohio,
where the merger happened in 1957, thirty people were elected, fifteen from
each of the two founding denominations, to develop a Statement of Faith.
Allen O. Miller refers to the Statement of Faith as "the wedding vows of our
two unifying churches,"[1] which brought together diverse histories and traditions.

The United Church of Christ Statement of Faith was born out of dedicated study
and prayer. Many parts of the Bible helped form the foundation it:

*The faith which unites us and to which we bear witness is that faith in God which
the Scriptures of the Old and New Testaments set forth, which the ancient church
expressed in the ecumenical creeds, to which our own spiritual [forebears] gave
utterance in the evangelical confessions of the Reformation, and which we are in
duty bound to express in the words of our time as God . . . gives us light.*[2]

From the very beginning of the United Church of Christ, the Statement of Faith
and other historical creeds were seen as ways to express faith in a given time
and place. The Statement of Faith was presented as a testimony to the faith of
the whole church, not as a test of faith for individual members.

After it was adopted by the Second General Synod in 1959 at Oberlin, Ohio, the Statement of Faith was offered to the whole church. Almost immediately local churches, associations, and conferences began to use the statement in creative ways in worship, study, and sermons. Since the original version was adopted, there have been two major revisions. In 1977, General Synod XI recommended a revision by Robert V. Moss Jr., then the president of the United Church of Christ, which used inclusive language, and in 1983 General Synod XIV affirmed a revision in the form of a doxology, addressing God as in prayer. That is the form that is used in *Affirming Faith*.

The Statement of Faith has a special place in the United Church of Christ. It is a powerful expression of God's saving acts and our invited response. It challenges Christians to "accept the cost and joy of discipleship, to be God's servants in the service of others, to proclaim the gospel to all the world and resist the powers of evil." Looking at the statement closely is an important step in discovering what it means to be a follower of Christ and a member of Christ's church.

Questions to Consider

THE SEVEN DECLARATIONS[3]

1. GOD CREATES

   You call the worlds into being, create persons in your own image, and set before each one the ways of life and death.

   Scripture: Genesis 1–3

   Questions: What does it mean to you to be created in God's image? In what ways are you a reflection of God?

2. GOD SEEKS TO SAVE

   You seek in holy love to save all people from aimlessness and sin.

   Scripture: John 3:16–21

   Questions: Have you ever known or experienced God's holy love? Have you ever experienced aimlessness? What does sin mean to you? How could God's love help save someone from being aimless?

3. **GOD JUDGES**

   You judge people and nations by your righteous will declared through prophets and apostles.

   Scripture: Hosea 2:16–20

   Questions: Have you ever been judged? How does God express judgment?

4. **GOD COMES TO US IN CHRIST**

   Jesus Christ, the man of Nazareth, our crucified and risen Savior, you have come to us and shared our common lot, conquering sin and death and reconciling the world to yourself.

   Scriptures: Acts 10:33–44, Philippians 2:5–11, Romans 3:21–26, 2 Corinthians 5:16–21

   Questions: What does it mean that God shares our common lot? How has Jesus shared this with us? What do you think are the ways of "sin and death" in our culture today? How does God's reconciling power challenge and conquer these?

5. GOD BESTOWS THE HOLY SPIRIT

You bestow upon us your Holy Spirit, creating and renewing the church of
Jesus Christ, binding in covenant faithful people of all ages, tongues, and races.

Scriptures: Acts 1–2, 1 Corinthians 12, Ephesians 4:1–6, 11–13

Questions: What does it mean for people of all ages, tongues, and races to be
bound together? How do you feel bound together with people of other ages,
tongues, or races? What could you or your congregation do to make the ties
even stronger?

6. GOD CALLS US TO DISCIPLESHIP

You call us into your church to accept the cost and joy of discipleship, to be
your servants in the service of others, to proclaim the gospel to all the world
and resist the powers of evil, to share in Christ's baptism and eat at his table, to
join him in his passion and victory.

Scriptures: Matthew 25:31–40, Mark 10:35–45, Matthew 28:19–20

Questions: In what ways do you or your church engage in service to others? In
what ways do you or your church resist the powers of evil?

7. GOD PROMISES

You promise to all who trust you forgiveness of sins and fullness of grace, courage in the struggle for justice and peace, your presence in trial and rejoicing, and eternal life in your realm which has no end.

Scriptures: Romans 12, Revelation 21:1–7

Question: How is a promise of courage in the struggle for justice and peace different from a promise of victory?

United Church of Christ Statement of Faith in the Form of a Doxology[4]

We believe in you, O God, Eternal Spirit,
God of our Savior Jesus Christ and our God,
and to your deeds we testify:
> *You call the worlds into being,*
>> *create persons in your own image,*
>> *and set before each one the ways of life and death.*
> *You seek in holy love to save all people from aimlessness*
> *and sin.*
> *You judge people and nations by your righteous will declared*
> *through prophets and apostles.*
> *In Jesus Christ, the man of Nazareth, our crucified and*
> *risen Savior,*
>> *you have come to us*
>> *and shared our common lot,*
>> *conquering sin and death*
>> *and reconciling the world to yourself.*
> *You bestow upon us your Holy Spirit,*
>> *creating and renewing the church of Jesus Christ,*
>> *binding in covenant faithful people of all ages,*
>> *tongues, and races.*
> *You call us into your church*
>> *to accept the cost and joy of discipleship,*
>> *to be your servants in the service of others,*
>> *to proclaim the gospel to all the world*
>> *and resist the powers of evil,*

to share in Christ's baptism and eat at his table,

to join him in his passion and victory.

You promise to all who trust you

forgiveness of sins and fullness of grace,

courage in the struggle for justice and peace,

your presence in trial and rejoicing,

and eternal life in your realm which has no end.

Blessing and honor, glory and power be unto you.

Amen.

United Church of Christ Statement of Faith Adapted by Robert V. Moss[5]

We believe in God, the Eternal Spirit, who is made known
to us in Jesus our brother, and to whose deeds we testify:

God calls the worlds into being,

creates humankind in the divine image,

and sets before us the ways of life and death.

God seeks in holy love to save all people from aimlessness
and sin.

God judges all humanity and all nations by that will of
righteousness declared through prophets and apostles.

In Jesus Christ, the man of Nazareth, our crucified and
risen Lord,

God has come to us

and shared our common lot,

conquering sin and death

and reconciling the whole creation to its Creator.

God bestows upon us the Holy Spirit,

     creating and renewing the church of Jesus Christ,

     binding in covenant faithful people of all ages,

     tongues, and races.

God calls us into the church

     to accept the cost and joy of discipleship,

     to be servants in the service of the whole

     human family,

     to proclaim the gospel to all the world

     and resist the powers of evil,

     to share in Christ's baptism and eat at his table,

     to join him in his passion and victory.

God promises to all who trust in the gospel

     forgiveness of sins and fullness of grace,

     courage in the struggle for justice and peace,

     the presence of the Holy Spirit in trial and rejoicing,

     and eternal life in that kingdom which has no end.

Blessing and honor, glory and power be unto God.

Amen.

Prayer

Thank you, God, for your loving action in the world. Help me to recognize your ways and testify to your deeds. Help me to trust you, and give you blessing and honor, glory and power. Amen.

Your Thoughts

_____

_____

_____

_____

_____

_____

_____

_____

_____

_____

_____

_____

_____

_____

1. Allen O. Miller, *The United Church of Christ Statement of Faith: A Historical, Biblical, and Theological Perspective* (New York: United Church of Christ, 1990), 9.
2. *Basis of Union of the Congregational Christian Churches and the Evangelical and Reformed Church with the Interpretations* 4, quoted in Roger L. Shinn, *Confessing Our Faith: An Interpretation of the Statement of Faith of the United Church of Christ* (New York: The Pilgrim Press, 1990), 9. The *Basis of Union* can be found in Louis H. Gunnemann, *The Shaping of the United Church of Christ* (New York: United Church Press, 1977), 208ff.
3. Biblical references come from Allen O. Miller, *The United Church of Christ Statement of Faith: A Historical, Biblical, and Theological Perspective* (New York: United Church Press, 1990), 13–15.
4. *United Church of Christ Book of Worship* (New York: Office for Church Life and Leadership, 1986), 514. Used by permission.
5. *The Statement of Faith* (inclusive-language version), revised by Robert V. Moss Jr., president of the United Church of Christ, 1969–76, and recommended for use by General Synod XI, 1977. Used by permission.

The creation of the whole universe and humanity is the work of God, the Eternal Spirit. All that God creates is good.

faith

GOD

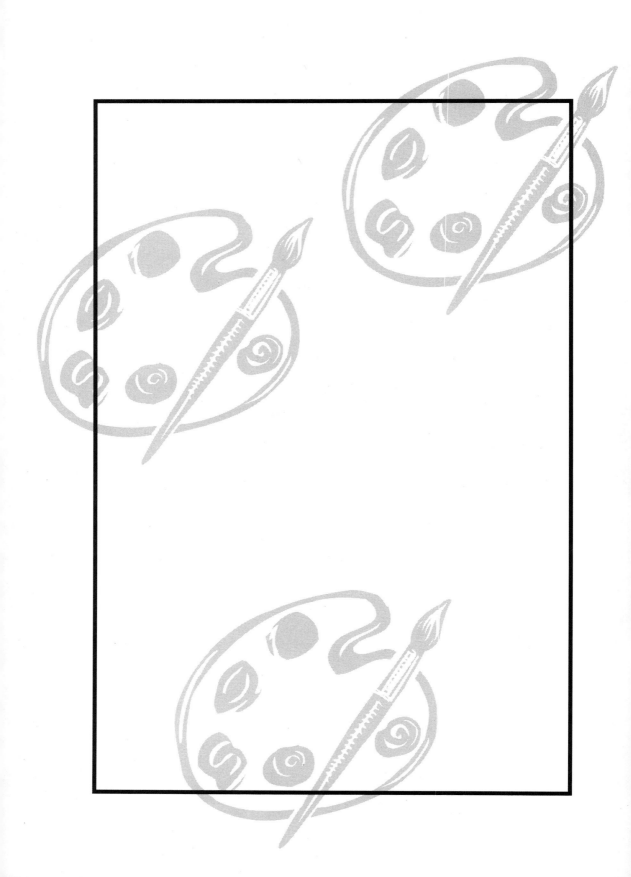

GOD CREATES

8

YOU CALL THE WORLDS INTO BEING, CREATE PERSONS IN YOUR OWN IMAGE,
AND SET BEFORE EACH ONE THE WAYS OF LIFE AND DEATH.

—STATEMENT OF FAITH

Themes

- The creation of the whole universe and humanity is the work of God, the Eternal Spirit.
- All that God creates is good.
- Humanity is made in the image of God.
- God gives humankind the capacity to choose the way of life.
- God calls humankind to be stewards of the Earth and part of the ongoing miracle of creation.

Scriptures

GENESIS 1:1–2:4A—At God's word the universe and humanity are created.

GENESIS 2:4B–25—God creates humankind from dust and gives the breath of life.

DEUTERONOMY 30:11–20—God sets before humankind the way of life and death and calls people to choose life.

Before You Gather

The creation stories from Genesis 1:1–2:4a and Genesis 2:4b–25 are two of the most familiar texts in the Bible, but they are often misunderstood. The confusion seems to arise from the fact that the stories are, at times, viewed as historical fact rather than as an affirmation of the creative power of God, the Eternal Spirit. The stories tell of the unfolding drama of the relation of the Creator to creation.

The power of God's word calls the worlds into being. God's sovereignty is supreme. God is active, birthing land, sea, and creature. "God's word is an act, an event, a sovereign command, which accomplishes a result. The creation story affirms that God's word, mighty in history, is also the very power which brought the creation into being."[1]

God takes dust and forms humankind. God breathes into humanity and gives the gift of life. Life is a gift, fashioned and molded, formed and created, valued and blessed by God. Humanity is a part of creation and yet is uniquely made in the image of God. God issues the call to humanity to live in God's world, to live with other creatures, and to live on God's terms.[2]

To be made in the image of God means we are given the gift to create. God entrusts us with an awesome gift. The responsibility is enormous, because we can create that which gives life or we can create that which leads to death. In Deuteronomy we hear God's call through the prophet Moses: "Choose life so that you and your descendants may live" (Deuteronomy 30:15, 19b).

As God's creation, made in God's image, we live with these unique qualities: our *creatureliness and dependence* and, in contrast, our *freedom and creativity*. One shows us our dependence upon our Creator for the gift of life. The other points to our capacity for choice in God's creation. With the gift of choice comes responsibility—as children of God, we are given creative powers to be stewards of creation and servants of peace and justice.[3] As stewards, we are to care for God's good creation with humility, reverence, and concern for the whole of creation.

For God, creation is an ongoing process with covenantal implications. God is known through acts of salvation, justice, and freedom. God creates, saves, and love. God is at work daily, renewing creation.

As those called to trust in God's purposes, we, too, can be renewed daily by God's creative Spirit. God calls us to life-giving actions, resisting the powers of death, so that creation will not be diminished. Even when we forget our call and turn away from God, God does not abandon us, but says, through the prophet Isaiah, "Do not fear, for I have redeemed you; I have called you by name, you are mine" (Isaiah 43:1).

Questions to Consider

@   What did you like best about the creation stories?

_____

_____

_____

_____

_____

@   What parts were the most challenging to you?

_____

_____

_____

_____

_____

ℓ How are these stories different from a scientific theory of creation?

_____

_____

_____

_____

_____

ℓ What do you suppose are the most important parts to remember about these

stories?

_____

_____

_____

_____

_____

ℓ What kind of love might God have for all that God has created?

_____

_____

_____

_____

_____

ℓ What hopes might God have for creation?

_____

_____

_____

_____

_____

@ What part do you think God wants humankind to play in making those hopes real?

_____

_____

_____

_____

_____

The Web of Life

God's creation was not a one-time event occurring long ago. It is ongoing, and even now we are part of it. Read and reflect on this poem attributed to Chief Seattle:

This we know. The earth does not belong to us, we belong to the earth. This we know. All things are connected like the blood which unites one family. All things are connected.

Whatever befalls the earth befalls the sons and daughters of the earth. We did not weave the web of life, we are merely a strand in it. Whatever we do to the web, we do to ourselves.[4]

Prayer

Creator God, the power of your word brought the worlds into being. You called your creation good. I am a part of that creation. You have created humankind in your image, and call us to be good stewards of creation. Help me to choose the things that give life and show my care for creation. Amen.

Your Thoughts

_____

_____

_____

_____

_____

_____

_____

_____

_____

_____

_____

_____

_____

_____

_____

1.   "Creation," *The Interpreter's Dictionary of the Bible*, vol. 1, ed. George A. Buttrick (Nashville: Abingdon Press, 1962), 728.
2.   Walter Brueggemann, *Genesis: A Bible Commentary for Teaching and Preaching* (Louisville: Westminster/John Knox 1982), 40.
3.   Allen O. Miller, *The United Church of Christ Statement of Faith: A Historical, Biblical, and Theological Perspective* (New York: United Church Press), 18–19.
4.   *Earth Prayers from Around the World*, ed. Elizabeth Roberts and Elias Amidon (San Francisco: HarperSan Francisco, 1991), 10. Used by permission of Elizabeth Roberts.

GOD SEEKS AND SAVES

YOU SEEK IN HOLY LOVE TO SAVE ALL PEOPLE FROM AIMLESSNESS AND SIN.

—STATEMENT OF FAITH

Themes

@ God seeks us in holy love, calling us into relationships based on wholeness and shalom.

@ Sin is a state of human life in which we are separated from one another, from ourselves, and from God.

@ Salvation is the gift of God's grace that frees us from sin, guilt, and the powers of death.

Scripture

ROMANS 5:12–21—Righteousness and life come from God's saving grace.

MARK 10:35–45—James and John seek honor.

MATTHEW 26:31–35, 69–75—Peter denies knowing Jesus.

JEREMIAH 2:4–13—God, through the prophet Jeremiah, accuses the people of turning against God.

Before You Gather

God seeks us in holy love, calling us into relationship. God has a call for everyone.
God's call, first and foremost, is to enter into a relationship—a deep, abiding
connection to God. Too often people respond to God as a distant being who
has little interest in them and who dictates rules and punishes them when they
do wrong. But as the Statement of Faith reminds us, God seeks in holy love to
save us from aimlessness and sin. Such a desire and action on God's part does
not imply God is a stern and distant disciplinarian, but rather a God who wants
to save us from this brokenness through relationship.

The "aimlessness and sin" from which God seeks to save us cannot be seen as
behaviors to avoid, nor as a list of immoral actions never to be done. Rather,
God desires that we live in shalom. *Shalom* is the Hebrew word meaning
wholeness, health, and deep and abiding peace. It is both a personal and corporate experience. A shalom person acts in ways that show God's love and grace.
A shalom society expresses God's justice and righteousness in its way in the
world. Sin is the absence of shalom.

In a famous sermon by theologian Paul Tillich called "You Are Accepted,"[1] Tillich
suggested a simple definition of sin: sin is separation.

There are three kinds of separation to which the word *sin* refers: separation
between people, separation of a person from him/herself, and separation of all
people from God. This threefold separation is one of the realities of life—it is a
universal fact, it is the fate of every life. To be human is to experience this separation. Before sin is an action, it is a way of being.

Think about how biblical people such as Abraham, Miriam, Moses, Jacob, Ruth,
Elizabeth, Mary, Peter, Paul, Anna, and Phoebe dealt with God—speaking,
negotiating, wrestling, even arguing in the most intimate ways. They knew
God to be as close to them as their closest friend.

God's call to us is not only to believe in God, but also to *love* God. This call does not come to us as a demand, but as an invitation. We are called to enter into a loving relationship with God, not because God will love us any less if we don't, but precisely because God has loved us first, and will always love us, no matter what we may do. Such unconditional love invites our love in return.

When we enter this relationship of love with God, it is likely that we will find ourselves beginning to value the very things God values and treasuring those God loves. Being in relationship with God leads us to want to do the things God finds pleasing. Consequently, in responding to God's love and saving grace, we become sensitive to God's concerns and respond to them so that God's own desires for justice and compassion are our desires too.

Questions to Consider

@ Think of a promise you have made or that was made to you. Was it kept or broken?

@ How does it feel to keep a promise? to break a promise? to get another chance?

@ Can you think of ways God has been with you in the past?

@ What is God calling or inviting you to do now in your life?

@ In what ways do you think God offers us help to live in relationships that are whole and loving?

Sin Is Separation

Name some of the ways we sin that separate us as we live our lives:

@   We separate from other people.

_____

_____

_____

_____

_____

_____

@   We separate from our own best intentions.

_____

_____

_____

_____

_____

_____

@   We separate from God.

_____

_____

_____

_____

_____

_____

_____

Reconciliation Is . . .

What does reconciliation mean to you? Draw or write it here.

A Time to Think

How would your life be the same or different if you took seriously the call to be in covenant with God?

_____

_____

_____

_____

_____

One Covenant

Here is one person's covenant. What do you think?

EARTH CREDO

> I believe in the sacredness of the earth,
>
> the integrity of the whole of creation and dignity
>
> of all people and creatures.
>
> I believe in a gracious God who created humankind—
>
> male and female, and gave them the responsibility
>
> to take care of the earth. We need to care.
>
> I believe we human beings have failed God and ourselves.
>
> In the name of greed and development
>
> we have dominated the earth.
>
> The people and creatures destroyed the forest,
>
> polluted the air, river and seas and have sacrificed
>
> the future of our children. We need to repent.
>
> I believe that when we destroy the earth,

we eventually destroy ourselves.

We must protect and preserve the earth not

only for our own survival but for the sake

of our mother earth. The time to change is now.

I believe we need to change our ways, values, lifestyle

and ways relating with creation.

Repent, fast and pray. Consume less, waste not.

Work for justice and peace.

We should not covet our neighbors' timber butterflies,

white sand beaches, nearly extinct animals nor cheap labor.

We should not oppress children, indigenous people,

women, the homeless, refugees and victims of war.

We need to live in the sense of people and creation.

For I believe in the interwovenness of life.

Creator and Creatures. Cosmic and Individual.

West, North, East, South. Rest and Prayer.

Food and Freedom. Theology and Ecology.

I therefore commit myself, together with you,

to take care for mother earth.

To advocate for peace and justice.

To choose and celebrate life.

These things I believe. Amen.

—*Elizabeth S. Tapia, Philippines*[2]

Write a Covenant

Here are some words that could begin a covenant with God. Use them or think of your own beginning for a covenant. Take some time to fill in your thoughts and ideas:

Because of the great love God has shown toward us, I hereby covenant to show my love for God by . . .

_____

_____

_____

_____

_____

_____

_____

_____

What are some concrete things you can do this coming week to live up to your covenant?

_____

_____

_____

_____

In one week and again in one month, review how you lived the covenant. Celebrate any success; forgive any failure. Know that God forgives you, and will support you in your attempt to live up to your covenant.

Prayer

Creator God, you give your love to all creation. As I receive your love, help me to share it with others. Amen.

Your Thoughts

\
\
\
\
\
\
\
\
\
\
\
\
\
\
\
\
\
\
\
\
\
\
\

1. See Paul Tillich, *Shaking the Foundations* (New York: Charles Scribner's Sons, 1948).
2. Elizabeth S. Tapia, from *A Time to Speak*, General Board of Global Ministries of the United Methodist Church and Youth and Young Adult Ministries, in coordination with the United Methodist Youth Fellowship in the Philippines and the Methodist Youth Fellowship in Korea, Manila, Philippines. Used by permission.

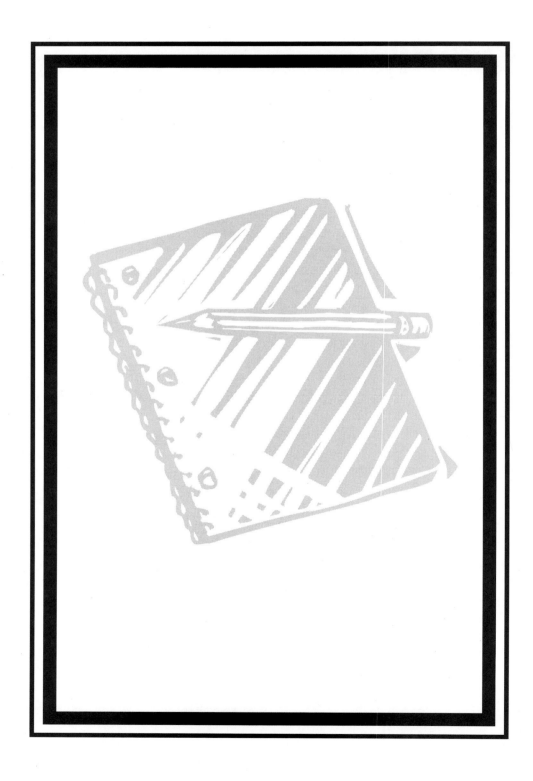

GOD LOVES AND JUDGES   **10**

YOU JUDGE PEOPLE AND NATIONS BY YOUR RIGHTEOUS WILL DECLARED THROUGH PROPHETS AND APOSTLES.

—STATEMENT OF FAITH

Themes

- God is a saving God who judges.
- God judges relationships with God, one another, ourselves, and the world by God's righteous will.
- There are times when we fail as individuals and as the church to be just and loving.

Scriptures

MICAH 6:6–8—Faithfulness to God is shown in acts of justice, kindness, and humility.

MATTHEW 25:31–40—What we do for others we do for Christ.

PSALM 130—God's love redeems.

Before You Gather

Micah 6:6–8 and Matthew 25:31–40 were written in different centuries and in times that were very different from our own, yet they describe relationships in a way that can help us today. Micah 6:6–8 tells us that God is more concerned about how we treat one another, ourselves, and God than in beautiful rituals or formal liturgies. Micah proclaimed that individual actions and relationships could make or break the entire society. He also affirmed that if the people would make loving and life-giving choices, their world would again be filled with joy. Eight centuries after Micah lived, Jesus' words in Matthew 25:31–40 echo the words of the prophet. Jesus tells us that the way we treat friends, family, and strangers is, in effect, the way we treat God.

Psalm 130 reminds us of God's unconditional love for us. Nothing we have done or ever could do will change that love. It also voices a prayer for deliverance, a cry for help and forgiveness in the midst of personal trouble. This scripture passage remind us that, although we may make unhealthy choices, God's choice is to love and care for us. God gives us the courage and strength to repair and restore our relationships.

Relationships consume lots of energy. Sometime relationships are sustaining and fulfilling. Others may be in conflict with the wholeness God desires for each person. Our faith journey is one that connects us to God's love and judgment. The journey begins with God calling us to accountability in our relationships with God, one another, and creation. Throughout the biblical story and our personal journeys we are faced with choices about how to answer that call. God is constantly encouraging us to make healthy and loving choices in our inter-actions with our world and God. Healthy choices in our relationships with God and one another must also include healthy choices in our relationships with the natural world, ourselves, and our communities. God encourages us to repair and rebuild relationships that are damaged. The journey is ongoing and the choices are always there for us to make. God's way offers hope for rec-onciliation.

Questions to Consider

Read Matthew 25:31–40. Jesus is saying that we may meet God in surprising places. Think about these questions and the questions below and write your answers in the space provided.

◎ Where have you unexpectedly seen the face of Christ? Was it at a time when you were helping or not helping another person? Explain.

_____

_____

_____

_____

_____

◎ Why would God care if we help the sick or feed the hungry or clothe the naked?

_____

_____

_____

_____

_____

◎ How might God expect faithful people and nations to act?

_____

_____

_____

_____

_____

@ What are some ways in which you make healthy and loving relationships with God, with yourself, with others, and with creation?

_____

_____

_____

_____

@ Recall a time when you hurt someone else and that person forgave you. How did it feel?

_____

_____

_____

_____

@ What have you learned about your relationship with God?

_____

_____

_____

Seeking Hope in God's Righteous Will

Is there a situation in your life or a situation in the world that needs God's healing or God's forgiveness? What it is? How might God's love and justice be known? Complete the following sentences:

@ I have a concern about . . .

_____

_____

_____

_____

@ It could be better if . . .

_____

_____

_____

_____

@ I think God would want . . .

_____

_____

_____

_____

@ I can show God's righteous will by . . .

_____

_____

_____

Prayer

Write a prayer to God describing any troubles or worries you are having. Ask God to help you with them. Then be open to the ways you and your troubles or worries might be changed with God's help in the week ahead.

_____

_____

_____

_____

_____

_____

_____

_____

_____

_____

_____

_____

_____

_____

_____

_____

_____

_____

_____

_____

Your Thoughts

God became
one of us in
the person
of Jesus of
Nazareth.

JESUS CHRIST

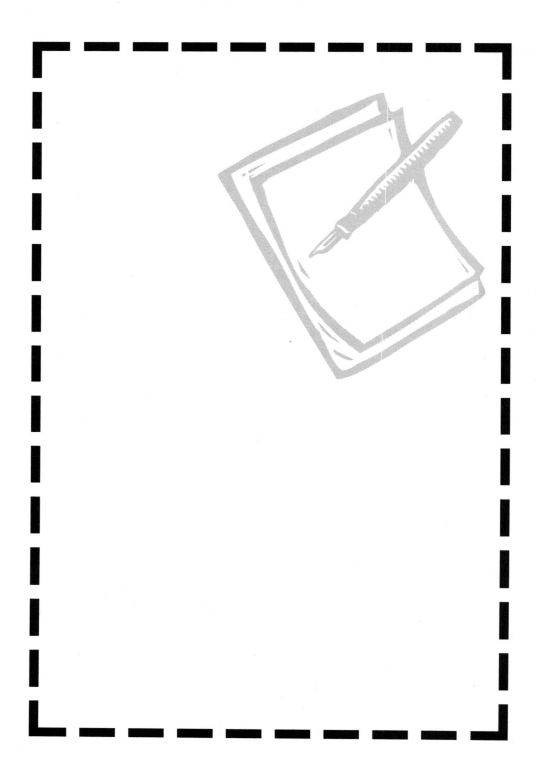

JESUS CHRIST,

HUMAN AND DIVINE

11

In Jesus Christ, the man of Nazareth, our crucified and risen Savior, you have come to us and share our common lot.

—Statement of Faith

Themes

@ Throughout history God has sought to relate to human beings.

@ God came to us in the person of Jesus of Nazareth.

@ Jesus' life expressed God in the world.

Scriptures

John 1:1–18—The Divine became human in Jesus Christ.

Luke 22:63–23:46—Jesus was physically hurt.

Mark 4:35–38—Jesus slept.

Matthew 21:18—Jesus was hungry.

John 11:28–36—Jesus wept for a friend.

Mark 6:30–32—Jesus spent time with his friends.

John 2:1–11—Jesus celebrated.

John 2:13–16—Jesus got angry.

Luke 2:41–51—Jesus upset his parents.

Matthew 15:30–38—Jesus felt sorry for someone else.

Before You Gather

From the beginning, God has looked for ways to relate to human beings. In Jesus Christ, God came to us and shared our common lot. This is to say that Jesus was both fully human and fully divine. Through the ages, groups of people in the church have argued about this. Some believed that Jesus was a great teacher, but only human, not divine. Other people believed that Jesus was really God in human form but not really human. From the early church to the present day, Christians have struggled to understand how Jesus could be fully human and fully divine at the same time.

Roger Shinn, in his book *Confessing Our Faith*, observes:

> *The Statement of Faith says: "In Jesus Christ, the man of Nazareth, our crucified and risen Savior, you [God] have come to us." That is, in this person Jesus, a genuine human being, you, the true God, have entered into our midst. You have not simply sent a messenger, a representative, but you . . . have entered the life of this person and through him the life of humankind.*[1]

Can you think of a time when you felt Christ's presence in your life? Maybe it was during prayer or while serving with other brothers and sisters in Christ on a project at church or in the community. God wants to be in our lives. Knowing God through Jesus Christ can help us in our relationship with God to sense God's love, strength, and support.

Questions to Consider

@ Why is it important to you that Jesus is truly God?

_____

_____

_____

@ Why is it important to you that Jesus was truly human?

_____

_____

_____

@ When I think of God coming to us and sharing our common lot I . . .

_____

_____

_____

@ When I think about Jesus Christ as a Savior I . . .

_____

_____

_____

The Parable of the Birds

Once upon a time there was a man who looked upon Christmas as a lot of humbug.

He wasn't a Scrooge. He was a very kind and decent person.

But he didn't believe all that stuff about an incarnation that churches proclaim at
Christmas. And he was too honest to pretend that he did. He simply could not

understand the claim that God became human. It didn't make any sense to him.

On Christmas Eve, his wife and children went to church for the midnight service, but he stayed home. It began to snow, "If we must have Christmas," he thought, "it's nice to have a white one." He sat down by the fire to read the newspaper. A few minutes later he heard a thudding sound, followed by another and another. Birds, caught in the storm, and in a desperate search for shelter, had tried to fly through his window. Now they lay huddled miserably in the snow. "I can't let the poor creatures lie there and freeze," he thought. "But how can I help them?"

He thought of the barn. It was a warm shelter. He put on his coat and overshoes and tramped out through the deepening snow to the barn. He opened the doors wide and turned on a light.

But the birds didn't come in.

"Food will bring them in," he thought. So he sprinkled a trail of bread crumbs from the birds to the sheltering barn.

To his dismay, the birds ignored the crumbs and continued to flop around helplessly in the snow.

He tried shooing them into the barn. They scattered in every direction—except the warm, lighted barn.

"They find me a strange and terrifying creature," he said to himself, "and I can't seem to think of any way to let them know they can trust me.

"If only I could be a bird myself for a few minutes, perhaps I could lead them to safety."

Just at that moment, the church bells began to ring. He stood silently for a while, listening to the bells pealing the glad tidings of Christmas.

Then he sank on his knees in the snow. "Now I do understand," he whispered. "Now I see why you had to do it."[2]

Prayer

Christ Jesus, help me to trust that you are always with me, even in the times when I doubt it or feel that I don't deserve your love. Amen.

Your Thoughts

_____

_____

_____

_____

_____

_____

_____

_____

_____

_____

_____

_____

_____

_____

_____

_____

_____

_____

_____

_____

1. Roger Shinn, *Confessing Our Faith* (New York: Pilgrim Press, 1990), 68–69.
2. Louis Cassells, "The Parable of the Birds," in *Advent: A Calendar of Devotions* (Nashville: Abingdon, 1976). Used by permission.

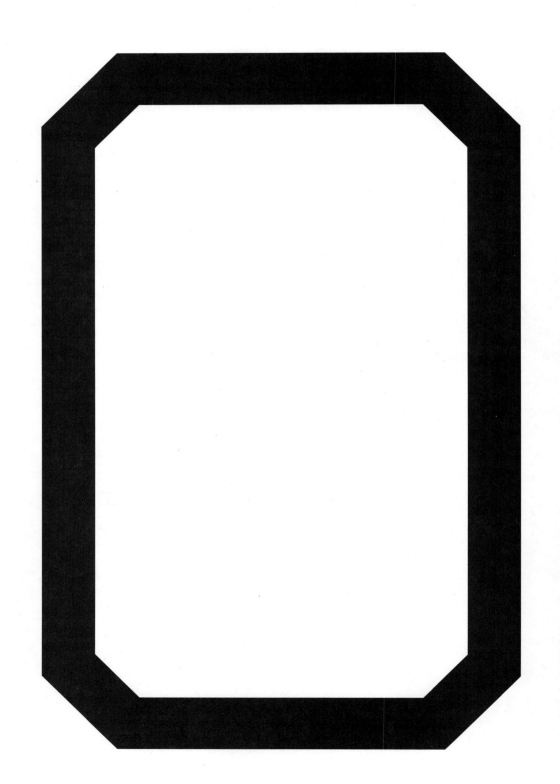

JESUS CHRIST,

CRUCIFIED AND RESURRECTED

12

IN JESUS CHRIST, . . . OUR CRUCIFIED AND RISEN SAVIOR, YOU HAVE COME TO US AND SHARED OUR COMMON LOT.

—STATEMENT OF FAITH

Themes

@ Jesus lived among us.

@ Jesus was crucified and resurrected.

@ Jesus' life and resurrection are central to the Christian faith.

@ Jesus Christ is present today in relationship.

Scripture

JOHN 18:1–20:31—The story of the crucifixion and resurrection is told.

Before You Gather

Whether you are considering the Christian faith for the first time or have been a Christian from earliest memory, there are few events for Christians that are more important or more difficult to understand than the crucifixion and resurrection. Why did Jesus die? What is the resurrection? What proof do we have in these matters? What does it mean that Jesus died for my sins and the sins of the world?

Over the past two thousand years, a variety of interpretations or explanations of the resurrection have been offered. There were some who believed that Jesus' disciples had secretly gone to the burial cave and stolen the body so they could claim that Christ had risen from the dead. There were others, called Gnostics, who claimed that Jesus was not really a human being like the rest of us. They said that his spirit was the only thing real about him and, since he wasn't alive in the same way that human beings are, he didn't experience death as human beings do. Another common belief in the Greek-Roman world was that the body and soul were separate, with the body serving merely as a house where the soul would live. This led to the idea for some that Jesus' spirit was resurrected, leaving his body behind.

None of these views were proclaimed by the early Christians. They simply told what they knew: the continuing presence of the risen Christ among them brought them out of hiding, freed them from their fears, and enabled them to proclaim God's love. As the Statement of Faith affirms, through the cross and the resurrection they experienced God sharing their "common lot, conquering sin and death." They proclaimed Jesus' resurrection as a unique event that demonstrated God's power over death once and for all.

John reports that the resurrected Jesus appeared to the fearful disciples, who had hidden themselves away from the Roman authorities and religious leaders. The disciples were afraid that the authorities might come seeking to execute them as well because they were followers of Jesus. The disciple Thomas, who was not present the first time Jesus appeared to the disciples, refused to believe Christ was risen until he could see Jesus with his own eyes and touch the wounds in Jesus' body. Once Thomas was convinced, however, he cried, "My Lord and my God!" (John 20:28). And Jesus' response to him underscores the mystery of the resurrection for the early church and for succeeding generations, "Have you believed because you have seen me? Blessed are those who have not seen and yet have come to believe" (John 20:29).

The gospel accounts reflect the view of the early church that Jesus' resurrection was a unique event that demonstrated God's power over sin and death once and for all. They affirmed the belief that Jesus' resurrection was a sure sign that they would be resurrected too.

Questions to Consider

@ Why do you think everyone abandoned Jesus during his trial and crucifixion?

_____

_____

@ Why do you think Jesus was crucified?

_____

_____

@ Do you feel any sympathy for Pontius Pilate, the chief priests, scribes, Pharisees, Judas, Peter, or Thomas? If so, why? If not, why not?

_____

_____

_____

@ What do you think Jesus meant when he said to Thomas, "Blessed are those who have not seen and yet believe" (John 20:29)?

_____

_____

_____

The Passion Story from John's Gospel

Paul T. Granlund, *Resurrection II,* cast bronze, 1973, as reproduced in *ARTS Advocate* (UCC Fellowship in the Arts) 12, no. 1 (winter 1990), cover. Used by permission.

@ John 18:1-27

This scene depicts Judas betraying Jesus into the hands of Roman soldiers and
Temple guards; Peter attempting to protect Jesus by cutting off the ear of the
high priest's slave; and Peter's denial that he was one of Jesus' followers. Jesus is
interrogated by Caiaphas before the Temple leaders, called the Sanhedrin.

@ John 18:28-19:16

Jesus is led away from the Sanhedrin to the praetorium, where Pilate asks Jesus'
accusers what charge they bring against him and then interrogates Jesus before
giving into the crowd's demand that Jesus be crucified.

@ John 19:17-42

This passage describes the crucifixion and burial of Jesus.

@ John 20:1-31

These verses describe Jesus' resurrection and the appearance of Jesus to the disciples, including his encounter with Thomas.

Prayer

God, you know me better than I know myself. Thank you for coming to us in Jesus so that I could have the opportunity to know you better. Amen.

Your Thoughts

_____

_____

_____

_____

_____

_____

_____

_____

_____

_____

_____

_____

_____

_____

_____

_____

_____

_____

_____

_____

JESUS CHRIST, RISEN SAVIOR

13

IN JESUS CHRIST, THE MAN OF NAZARETH, OUR CRUCIFIED AND RISEN SAVIOR, YOU HAVE COME TO US . . . CONQUERING SIN AND DEATH AND RECONCILING THE WORLD TO YOURSELF.

—STATEMENT OF FAITH

Themes

- Jesus Christ is Sovereign and Savior.
- Jesus Christ delivers the world from sin, death, and oppression.
- Jesus Christ restores a right relationship between humanity and God, among persons, and with all of creation.

Scriptures

JOHN 1:29–34—Jesus takes away the sin of the world.

2 CORINTHIANS 5:16–21—God calls us to be reconcilers.

Before You Gather

Jesus was born into a mix of despair, frustration, fear, and confusion. He grew up when times were difficult and uncertain. Most people were poor. Many who were well-off did little to help the less fortunate. Many people suffered from mental or physical illness or disabilities; others were homeless and hungry. In those days there were few cures; people died from diseases and malnutrition. Some of the religious leaders taught that people were sick or poor because they did not live according to God's law or will. Some believed that people were to blame for their situations.

The Jewish people lived under the rule of the Roman Empire—they were oppressed, heavily taxed, and treated cruelly. The vast majority of the people were looked down upon by those who were wealthy and had power. Ordinary citizens, Jews and Gentiles (non-Jews), young and old, were afraid of both government officials and religious leaders. They felt helpless and hopeless. They had no power—economically, socially, or politically. They lived at the margins of society and yearned for freedom and dignity.

Many of the people longed for a savior, someone who they hoped would rescue them from their lowly status. During his ministry, Jesus taught about the reign of God that would transform peoples' lives. Some people, then as now, believed this meant social reform and a politically dominant religious government. Others longed for a place of peace and tranquility. Still others recognized that Jesus offered a new way to live in the midst of all that works against them, even while maintaining hope in the future.

Jesus taught that the reign of God comes as a miracle and as a gift. Signs of God's reign included healing, offering forgiveness and blessing, and having fellowship with outcasts. Jesus' actions demonstrated that God's reign was present: he healed people—the sick, the lame, the blind, and those possessed by evil spirits; he ate with sinners, gluttons, and tax collectors, who were despised by most people; he listened to women and others who were given few opportunities or power in his society to express their ideas and perspectives.

In the Second Letter to the Corinthians, Paul describes the new life that Christ revealed as a transformed reality, a "new creation" (5:17). He equates the new creation with the reconciliation of all people to God. Jesus has shown us how to live and has drawn us back to God's will.

One of the greatest signs of God's reign was God saying no to the powers of death by way of the resurrection. In Christ's death and resurrection God met death and exposed its weakness. Christ's resurrection says that death has no lasting power and that people are free to live a new life. The resurrection was God's great act of salvation for the entire universe.

In the Statement of Faith, the verbs *conquering* and *reconciling* are in the present tense. This was done intentionally to indicate that, through Christ, God continues to conquer sin and reconcile creation and calls us through the ministry of reconciliation to "become the righteousness of God" (2 Corinthians 5:21).

Reconciliation Is . . .

_____

_____

_____

_____

The Meaning of Reconciliation

Allan Boesak, a leader in the movement that ended apartheid (racial segregation) in South Africa, reflected on the cost of discipleship in the context of the church in South Africa and defined reconciliation this way: "Reconciliation is not feeling good; it is coming to grips with evil. In order to reconcile, Christ had to die. We must not deceive ourselves. Reconciliation does not mean holding hands and singing: 'black and white together.' It means rather, death and suffering, giving up one's life for the sake of the other."[1]

Questions to Consider

@ What does it mean to you to show reconciliation?

_____

_____

_____

@ What is most difficult about reconciliation?

_____

_____

_____

@ What makes reconciliation important?

_____

_____

_____

@ How did Jesus show reconciliation?

_____

_____

_____

@ How would you go about the process of reconciliation?

_____

_____

_____

Litany: Questions of the Candidate[2]

Confirmands: *Do you desire to affirm your baptism into the faith and family of Jesus Christ?*

Leader(s): *I do.*

Confirmands: *Do you renounce the powers of evil and desire the freedom of new life in Christ?*

Leader(s): *I do.*

Confirmands: *Do you profess Jesus Christ as Lord and Savior?*

Leader(s): *I do.*

Confirmands: *Do you promise, by the grace of God, to be Christ's disciple, to follow in the way of our Savior, to resist oppression and evil, to show love and justice, and to witness to the work and word of Jesus Christ as best you are able?*

Leader(s): *I promise, with the help of God.*

Confirmands: *Do you promise, according to the grace given you, to grow in the Christian faith and to be a faithful member of the church of Jesus Christ, celebrating Christ's presence and furthering Christ's mission in all the world?*

Leader(s): *I promise, with the help of God.*

2 Corinthians 5:17

So if anyone is in Christ, there is a new creation: everything old has passed away; see, everything has become new!

Prayer

By your love, O God, I know that I am special and have a place in the church, the body of Christ. By following Jesus' example, may I also be an example to others as I depend on your help to resist the powers of evil and work for peace in the world. Amen.

Your Thoughts

_____

_____

_____

_____

_____

_____

_____

_____

_____

_____

_____

_____

_____

_____

_____

_____

_____

_____

_____

1.   Allan Boesak, *Black and Reformed* (Maryknoll, N.Y.: Orbis Books, 1984), 290.
2.   *United Church of Christ Book of Worship* (New York: Office for Church Life and Leadership, 1986), 149. Used by permission.

The Holy Spirit
creates,
nurtures,
and helps
us use our
gifts for the
good of all
creation.

THE HOLY SPIRIT

GUIDED BY THE SPIRIT

You bestow upon us your Holy Spirit, creating and renewing the church of Jesus Christ.

—Statement of Faith

Themes

- The Holy Spirit is a part of the great mystery of the Trinity.
- The Holy Spirit creates, nurtures, and helps us use our gifts for the good of all creation.
- The Holy Spirit works through the church.

Scriptures

John 16:1–7—Jesus promises that the Advocate (Holy Spirit) will come to the disciples.

John 20:19–23—The risen Christ offers peace to the disciples and gives them the gift of the Holy Spirit.

Galatians 5:13–26—Living by the Spirit produces fruit of the Spirit.

1 Corinthians 12:4–11—There are varieties of gifts, but the same Spirit is in everyone for the common good.

Before You Gather

The Holy Spirit comes in many different ways and works through the lives of people in a variety of circumstances. The Holy Spirit may be the common bond that enables us to experience kinship with, and a respect for, all people of every faith. Every human being has access to the Holy Spirit, yet the Spirit "blows where it chooses" (John 3:8), often where we least expect it.

Christians use the name Holy Spirit, which we believe to be the third person of the Trinity—both the Spirit of God and the Spirit given by Christ. This Spirit is both inside of us and all around us. The Holy Spirit strengthens and sustains us and empowers the work and worship of the church.

The Hebrew word *ruach* or *ruah*, like the Greek word *pneuma*, can mean "wind" or "breath" as well as "spirit." In the beginning, the Spirit or Wind of God swept over the face of the waters (Genesis 1:2) and gave us the breath of life (2:7). Continuing this word play, Jesus says to Nicodemus, "The wind blows where it chooses, and you hear the sound of it, but you do not know where it comes from or where it goes. So it is with everyone who is born of the Spirit" (John 3:8).

The scriptures for this session show how the Holy Spirit comes in many different forms and works through the lives of people in a variety of circumstances. The Spirit does not take us out of the struggles of our world or our lives. Instead, we are provided with a Spirit that gives us gifts and talents to share with the world and helps us in all of our struggles. Through our struggles, we are to take care of one another, and we are to take care of God's creation.

Gathering Prayer

O Great Spirit, whose voice I hear in the winds, and whose breath gives life to all the world, hear me! I am small and weak, I need your strength and wisdom. . . . Make me always ready to come to you with clean hands and straight eyes. So when life fades, as the fading sunset, my spirit may come to you without shame.

—Traditional Native American Prayer[1]

Questions to Consider

❧ What are some traditional places where people go to experience the presence of the Holy Spirit?

_____

_____

_____

_____

❧ Where have you experienced the presence of the Spirit?

_____

_____

_____

_____

❧ How do you sense the Spirit moving within you?

_____

_____

_____

_____

Gifts Inventory

To help you discover your gifts, think about the things that you:

@ love to do

@ do well

@ make you feel satisfied or proud

Write your responses. Then consider each of the following questions and write your answers in the space provided. Remember, these are your personal notes. You will share with others only what you want to share.

@ What gifts has the Spirit given you personally?

@ Which gifts do you share with others? How? Where? When? With whom?

@ Which gifts do you withhold? How? From whom? Why?

@ What gifts has the Spirit given us as a community of faith?

@ How do we share them with others? How do we withhold them?

@ What would free us to share our gifts more fully?

@ Who is withholding gifts that you think are worth sharing? How could you help that person to share his or her gifts more fully? Who else could help?

Create an Expression of the Holy Spirit

❷ Write a story or poem about a time when you felt the Holy Spirit was with you.

❷ Draw a picture that represents the Holy Spirit bringing unity in diversity.

❷ Write a prayer that asks the Holy Spirit to address a concern you have for the world.

Centering Prayer

Close your eyes and listen to the sound of your own breathing. Feel the action of your breath entering and leaving your lungs. How are breath and wind related? (Both are air.) How are they like the Spirit?

Many Christians practice the discipline of prayer using the centering prayer. As you breath in, imagine the Spirit of God filling your life. As you breath out, imagine the Spirit of God going out into the world through you and other Christians. Try a centering prayer, focusing on your breathing for several minutes.

Write a brief prayer thanking God for who you are and for the help of the Spirit in being who you are.

_____

_____

_____

_____

_____

_____

_____

_____

_____

_____

_____

_____

_____

_____

_____

Prayer

Thank you, God, for the Holy Spirit. I pray that I will understand how the Spirit seeks to guide and lead me. Help me to be open to the ways I can follow. Amen.

Your Thoughts

_____

_____

_____

_____

_____

_____

_____

_____

_____

_____

_____

_____

_____

_____

_____

_____

_____

_____

_____

_____

1. Elizabeth Roberts and Elias Amidon, eds., *Earth Prayers from Around the World* (San Francisco: HarperCollins, 1991), 188. Used by permission.

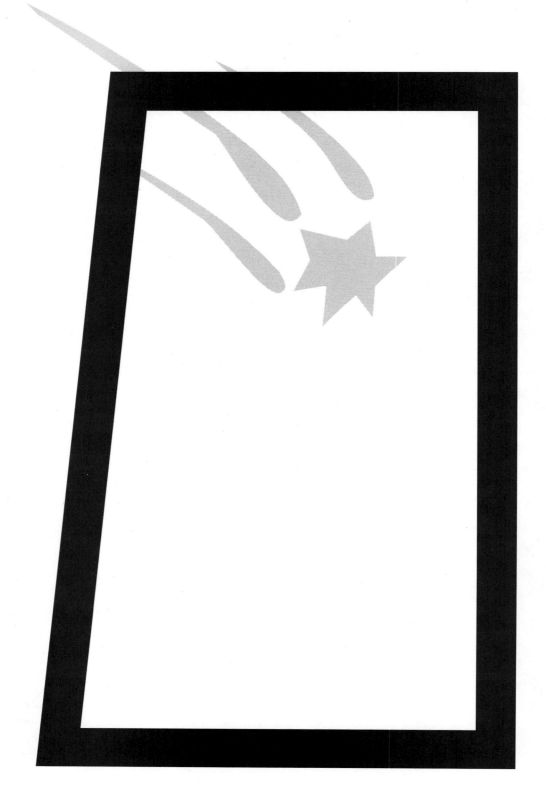

BOUND BY THE SPIRIT

YOU BESTOW UPON US YOUR HOLY SPIRIT, . . . BINDING IN COVENANT PEOPLE
OF ALL AGES, TONGUES, AND RACES.

—STATEMENT OF FAITH

Themes

- The Holy Spirit works in and through each of us.
- The Holy Spirit unites us in our diversity.

Scriptures

JEREMIAH 31:31–34—God's covenant is written on human hearts.

1 CORINTHIANS 11:23–25—Paul describes the new covenant in Christ's blood.

ACTS 2:1–24—Jesus' followers were filled with the Holy Spirit and began to speak
in many languages.

ACTS 2:37–47—Peter called the people to repentance, and the early Christians
became a community.

Before You Gather

The church is a covenant people. A covenant is an agreement made by two or
more people or groups.[1] The church has understood covenant as an agreement

between God and God's people. The concept of covenant was fundamental to the faith of the Hebrew people, and it remains important for those of us who call ourselves Christian. Our covenant in Christ helps us unite with God, others, and creation despite our differences.

The different "tongues" in the Pentecost story are not only vehicles of communication but are also symbols of different ways of looking at life. The story of Pentecost affirms that the reality of God cannot be expressed in just one way.

No group can claim to have special possession of the blessings of God. God's blessings come to all. When we truly receive God's blessings, we find that human differences—between men and women, young and old, those served and those serving, differently abled persons, those with various racial and ethnic backgrounds—no longer control our relationships in negative ways.

The Holy Spirit is present when there is space to see God in many different ways. These can change our understandings and actions. Where inequalities are overcome, the Spirit of God is present. Where solidarity and concern for the well-being of others is our main concern, the Spirit of God is working.

The Meaning of Covenant

It is important for the church to remember the nature of its belief about the covenant. The Christian covenant is not simply an agreement between consenting people, who are free to break it by mutual agreement. It is a covenant between people of faith and God, the Creator and Renewer of the church.[2]

—Roger Shinn

Questions to Consider

✑ What does it mean to you to be bound together by the Spirit?

_____

_____

✑ How could you express this in a letter, a poem, a song, or a drawing?

_____

_____

Bound Together in the Spirit

In 1985, on a trip to El Salvador, I had the occasion to visit the large, downtown cathedral of the Archdiocese of San Salvador. It was an unfinished edifice and had been turned into a haven for refugees by Archbishop Oscar Romero. I entered the cathedral and began interacting with the people who had been left homeless in their own country. When I noticed a young boy sitting off by himself, I went over to him, sat down, and spoke a greeting in Spanish. The boy immediately began feeling and touching me, and I soon realized that he was blind. In a very adultlike manner, he said, "I am blind, but I know you have come in peace." Then, almost instantly, he became a child again. "Do you think I will be safe here?" he asked. I searched for a reply and finally answered, "I can think of no safer place than the house of God." As I reflect on that exchange with a frightened child, I am convinced that the house of God should be a place for all God's people to feel safe and free—an all-inclusive, secure, accepting, and liberating space.[3]

—Daniel F. Romero

Prayer

Thank you, God, for a church that is made richer by the gifts of people of different ages, cultures, abilities, skills, and talents. Guide me by your Holy Spirit and bind me together in covenant with your faithful people in all times and places. Amen.

Your Thoughts

_____

_____

_____

_____

_____

_____

_____

_____

_____

_____

_____

_____

_____

_____

_____

_____

_____

_____

1. *Webster's New World Dictionary of the American Language, 2nd College Edition* (New York: Simon & Schuster, 1984), 326.
2. Roger L. Shinn, *Confessing Our Faith: An Interpretation of the Statement of Faith of the United Church of Christ* (New York: The Pilgrim Press, 1990), 83.
3. Daniel F. Romero, *Our Futures Inextricably Linked: A Vision of Pluralism* (Cleveland, Ohio: United Church Board for Homeland Ministries Division of Education and Publication, 1995), 7.

What is the church? The church is the body of Christ, with individual members working together as one body.

THE CHURCH

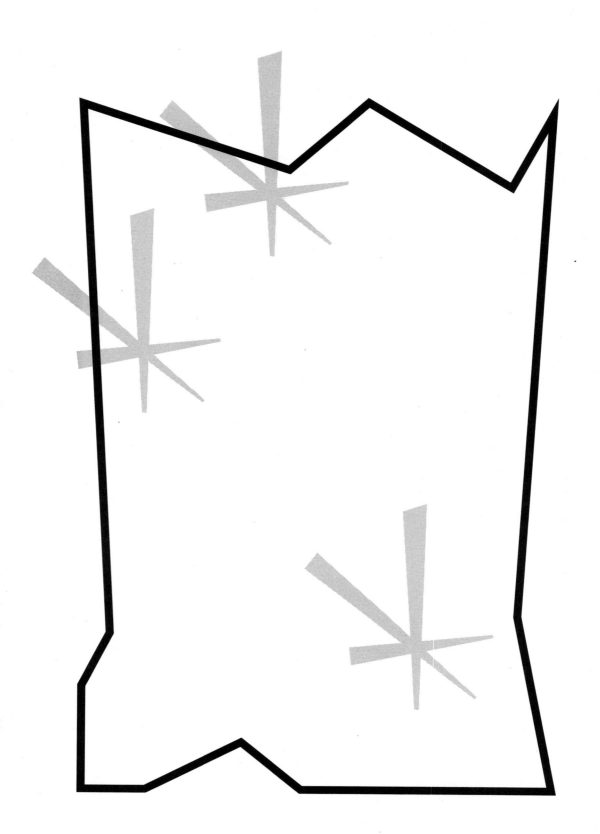

THE BODY OF CHRIST

Themes

@ The church is the body of Christ.

@ Christians participate in ministries of worship, teaching, and service.

Scriptures

1 CORINTHIANS 12:12–27—The church is the body of Christ.

ROMANS 12:1–8—Paul outlines the way believers are to live as the body of Christ.

1 TIMOTHY 4:11–16—Paul instructs Timothy in the way to teach about Christ.

EPHESIANS 4:1–16—Unity in the body of Christ is the ideal.

Before You Gather

The church is the body of Christ. The phrase "body of Christ" is a metaphor, in which Paul describes people in the church as being parts of a body. We are different and have different skills and gifts to offer one another. When we all do our part, the body is healthy and whole. When one or more of us does not participate as we are able, the whole body suffers.

Jesus Christ is the head of the church and we are the body. As the body of Christ, we are called to worship God, to learn more about God through Jesus Christ, and to minister in Christ's name. This body attempts to continue to live as Christ did, spreading a gospel of love, peace, and justice.

The church has many ministries carried out by its members. Three essential ministries are: a ministry of worship, a ministry of teaching and learning, and a ministry of service. These three ministries provide a foundation for seekers of the faith to explore, deepen, and live out their understanding of God.

God gives us gifts and we are called to use these gifts to build up the body of Christ (the church) and the world. Believing and following Jesus Christ includes striving to minister not only within the Christian community, but in the world as well. Through worship, teaching, and service, we may begin to discover that our lives are a part of a larger whole related to a source of power beyond ourselves. We may gain a better understanding of who God is and what God is calling us to be and do in the world. And we may be able to witness God's love more fully.

Gifts Bingo

Look at the gifts and qualities named in each square. Seek persons in the group who possess these gifts or qualities. Ask them to write their initials in the square.

kind	truthful	good listener	good helper
fair	patient	caring leader	imaginative
resists evil	seeks justice	peacemaker	assertive
creative	empowers others	keeps promises	loyal

Questions to Consider

⊚ Tell about an experience in worship that was meaningful for you. What happened that made it meaningful? How did it connect you with other Christians?

_____

_____

_____

⊚ Name at least three things that you have learned about faith while you have been involved in some church-sponsored activity.

_____

_____

_____

⊚ What have you taught others about God or faith, either formally or informally, at church?

_____

_____

⊚ What have you taught others about God or faith, either formally or informally, in some setting other than the church?

_____

_____

⊚ What talents or abilities did you share in some way this past week because you are a follower of Christ?

_____

_____

Litany

One: *For the talents and abilities that we have,*

All: *We thank you God.*

One: *For the faith that stirs and grows in our hearts,*

All: *We thank you God.*

One: *When we doubt your presence during difficult days,*

All: *Help us to trust in you.*

One: *When we are afraid to be who we really are,*

All: *Help us to trust in you.*

One: *As we risk sharing ourselves with others,*

All: *Be with us, O God.*

One: *As we receive what others have to give us,*

All: *Be with us, O God.*

Prayer

God, you call us to be the body of Christ. In a world filled with more and more ideas about how to live life, show me the ways in which following Christ can give special meaning to my life and make your reign known in the world. Amen.

Your Thoughts

_____

_____

_____

_____

_____

_____

_____

_____

_____

_____

_____

_____

_____

_____

_____

_____

_____

_____

_____

FOLLOWERS OF CHRIST

17

YOU CALL US INTO YOUR CHURCH . . . TO ACCEPT THE COST AND JOY OF DISCIPLESHIP.

—STATEMENT OF FAITH

Themes

- Following Christ is a lifelong commitment.
- Following Christ has a cost.
- Following Christ brings great joy.

Scriptures

JOHN 21:15–17—The risen Christ commands Peter to care for God's people.

MATTHEW 4:18–22—Jesus meets two fishers and challenges them to follow.

MARK 8:34–35—Jesus gives the ultimate challenge of discipleship: take up the cross.

LUKE 8:1–3—Mary Magdalene, Joanna, and Susanna follow Jesus as he proclaims the good news of God's reign.

Before You Gather

For the first disciples, the difficulties and sacrifices of following Christ were real. Jesus asked them to do no less than leave their work and life to become part of a ministry that changed the world. The call to discipleship is not limited by gender, race, sexual orientation, class, or ability. Long after the resurrection, Christ's call reaches out to people from diverse backgrounds.

The cost of discipleship can be summed up in Jesus' words: "If any want to become my followers, let them deny themselves and take up their cross and follow me. For those who want to save their life will lose it, and those who lose their life for my sake, and for the sake of the gospel, will save it" (Mark 8:34–35). It means living fully with love for ourselves and others. It means seeking ways to serve with integrity. It means caring for and loving others. It means reaching out with love to all people, of different races, cultures, and life experiences.

There is also joy and peace of mind when followers of Jesus look to the fulfillment of God's promise. The prophet Isaiah spoke of such a time of joy, when "the wolf shall dwell with the lamb" and "the earth shall be full of the knowledge of God" (Isaiah 11:6–9). In these days of chaos—hate, violence, wars, famine, disasters—there is hope that a day is coming when God shall "wipe away every tear" (Revelation 7:16–17).

Questions to Consider

The words *disciple* and *discipline* come from the same root. Think about something you really like to do that you get better at by doing or practicing, for example, art, music, a game or sport, riding a bike, cooking. Try to remember the first time, or first few times, you did it.

- How was it? What did you notice about your progress? How did it feel?
- How did your commitment to this discipline fit in with other important things in your life? What did you do? What was that like?
- What parts of the process were most enjoyable? What parts were least enjoyable?
- What kind of commitment did it take to learn how to do it? Did it bring you joy?

Draw or write about your answers and reflections.

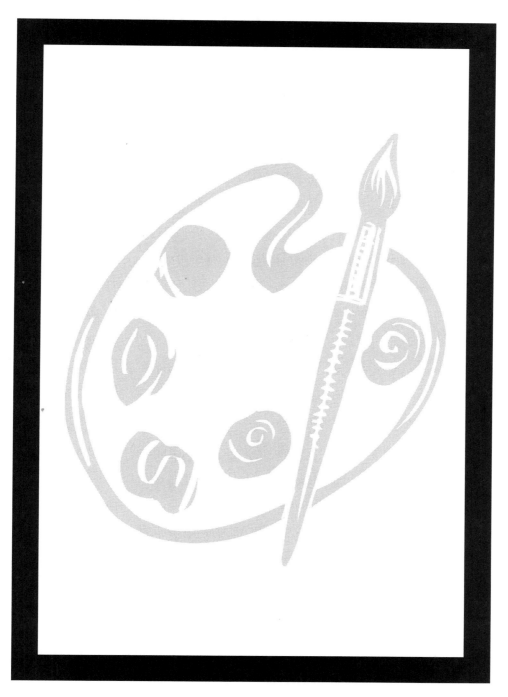

Qualities of a Disciple

One of the modern-day disciples of Jesus, Dietrich Bonhoeffer, the Lutheran pastor and leader of the Confessing Church in Germany fighting against Hitler and the terror of the Nazis, gives us a picture of the cost of discipleship. He wrote about the characteristics of Jesus' disciples based on the Beatitudes (Matthew 5:3–12):

@ Jesus' disciples are poor in spirit (they accept privation for Jesus' sake).

@ Jesus' disciples are those who mourn (who mourn the guilt of the world and its fate, and bear sorrow and suffering for the sake of the world).

@ Jesus' disciples are meek (they renounce their own lives to follow Christ).

@ Jesus' disciples hunger and thirst for righteousness.

@ Jesus' disciples are merciful.

@ Jesus' disciples are peacemakers.

@ Jesus' disciples are persecuted for righteousness sake.[1]

Discipleship Survey

For two or three days, keep a log of how you spend your time: school, eating, sleeping, hanging out, and so on. If you find keeping the log fun, continue through the week. Pay special attention to all the things you do that are acts of discipleship—reaching out to people or animals or other parts of creation with the same care and love Christ shows us. Also add the helping things you do for others that you have to do, like caring for a younger sibling or taking out the trash. These may or may not be acts of discipleship depending on where your heart is and what your motives for helping are.

Record your activities beginning on the next page. Write down all of them so that you get a sense of how much of your total time is spent in discipleship activities. Use the lines marked "Cost" and "Joy" to describe your thoughts and feelings about the activities that you have to do, you want to do, or feel moved to do by your own sense of care and compassion. Use blank paper if you need additional space to log your activities.

ACTIVITY Take care of younger brother.

COST I miss doing things with my friends.

JOY I can show my love for my brother.

ACTIVITY Help in the tutoring program.

COST I have to get up early to get there on time.

JOY It is fun to see others learn.

ACTIVITY Wash the dishes.

COST It is not much fun.

JOY I like to help my family this way.

ACTIVITY _____

COST _____

JOY _____

ACTIVITY _____

COST _____

JOY _____

ACTIVITY _____

COST _____

JOY _____

ACTIVITY _____

COST _____

JOY _____

ACTIVITY _____

COST _____

JOY _____

ACTIVITY _____

COST _____

JOY _____

ACTIVITY _____

COST _____

JOY _____

ACTIVITY _____

COST _____

JOY _____

ACTIVITY _____

COST _____

JOY _____

ACTIVITY _____

COST _____

JOY _____

ACTIVITY _____

COST _____

JOY _____

ACTIVITY _____

COST _____

JOY _____

ACTIVITY _____

COST _____

JOY _____

ACTIVITY _____

COST _____

JOY _____

ACTIVITY _____

COST _____

JOY _____

ACTIVITY _____

COST _____

JOY _____

ACTIVITY _____

COST _____

JOY _____

Prayer

Dear Jesus, I know there will be costs and joys when I follow you. Help me to experience your unconditional love, so that I may find the strength I need to serve you. Amen.

Your Thoughts

_____

_____

_____

_____

_____

_____

_____

_____

_____

_____

_____

_____

_____

_____

_____

_____

_____

_____

_____

1.   Adapted from Dietrich Bonhoeffer, *The Cost of Discipleship,* rev. ed. (New York: Macmillan, 1959), 95ff.

WITNESS AND SERVICE

18

YOU CALL US INTO YOUR CHURCH . . . TO BE YOUR SERVANTS IN THE SERVICE OF OTHERS, TO PROCLAIM THE GOSPEL TO ALL THE WORLD AND RESIST THE POWERS OF EVIL.

—STATEMENT OF FAITH

Themes

- A disciple of Jesus Christ is an active servant in the world.
- Faith is made real through one's choices and actions.
- Choosing life and resisting evil are part of discipleship.

Scriptures

JAMES 2:14–17—Faith and works together bring life.

JOHN 13:3–15—Jesus washes the disciples' feet.

MATTHEW 28:16–20—Jesus sends the disciples out to the nations.

1 JOHN 3:17–18—God's love calls for words and action.

Before You Gather

The disciples experienced Jesus' ministry. They were firsthand witnesses to Jesus' preaching, teaching, and healing. Through his words and actions the disciple began to understand the new relationship that Jesus came to establish between humanity and God.

Jesus encouraged the disciples to be witnesses to God's love to the world and to live as faithful people acting on their own understanding of God's love. The disciples were sent to be witnesses of Jesus Christ through words and actions so that others might also become believers.

Lives can be changed when persons see the love of God made real in other persons. Family, friends, teachers, peers, and even strangers can help shape and influence how you live your life. Action, which makes one's devotion to Christ real, is at the center of faith formation. Christianity's power emerges in the world when followers not only "talk the talk, but also walk the walk."

Stories of Witness and Service

ST. GEORGE'S

St. George's United Church in Johannesburg, South Africa, is a multiracial, inner-city church with about four hundred members. Rev. Diane Wicks, a United Church of Christ/Christian Church (Disciples of Christ) missionary serving the parish, describes it as a church "seeking to be a model church for the new South Africa, bridging the gap between community and church concerns and to be a place where all are welcome, struggling together to bring about God's vision for us."

Every Sunday night, church volunteers staff a soup kitchen that serves over two hundred people. Another program called the Community Outreach Ministry reaches out to homeless and unemployed people in the city. Diane has developed a newspaper called *Homeless Talk*, written and distributed by the homeless. The newspaper provides an income for the homeless and a way to tell their stories. One story was written by Johnannes Vusi Mavuka. He says:

"The fundamental cause of my suffering was not finding a permanent employment
after leaving school. I stayed with my aunt, who was a pensioner (on a fixed
income). I left when I felt I was a burden. I had to face the outside world
unarmed, with no qualifications, no accommodation, and no finance. My heart
was filled with bitterness and vengeance. During this period I met some people
with the same problems and resorted to gangsterism and joined some bad company. Then I befriended Rev. Diane from St. George's and my life changed. We
shared problems and ideas. I became interested in the Bible. I was encouraged
by quotes like, 'Seek God first and all others will be added to you.' That was
happening to me. Now I know the meaning of love and caring."[1]

LA FAMILIA

La Familia is the name of a United Church of Christ new church start in Paterson,
New Jersey, that has grown from 30 in the first year to 120, most of whom are
children. The pastor, Rev. Cruz Echevarria, talks about the significance of the
church's name.

"To the Hispanic people that means a lot because we try to keep the family very
tight. We have been working with people who are in real need. We have a
ministry with single mothers and with young people who have become our
evangelists. They feel the love of the church because we are very caring and
concerned about people."[2]

DEACONESS HEALTH SYSTEM

Rev. Deborah Patterson is the minister of religion and health at the United Church
of Christ–related Deaconess Incarnate Word Health System in St. Louis,
Missouri. Its mission is to foster a life of quality for all through value-centered
health care and health education offered in the compassionate spirit of Jesus
Christ.

Deborah describes the history of Deaconess: "We began our healing ministry in 1889 when the Evangelical Deaconess Society founded Deaconess Hospital because of the great need for quality health care to serve the poor and immigrant population in the St. Louis area."

Today Deaconess Incarnate Word Health System provides home health care, hospice, parish nursing, and other outpatient services at a variety of sites around St. Louis, and acute care at three hospitals. It has a nursing school and teaching hospitals for osteopathic and allopathic physicians. Deaconess's 1995 merger with Incarnate Word Hospital, sponsored by the Roman Catholic Sisters of Charity of the Incarnate Word, has been an important ecumenical partnership. The work of the hospitals reflects the combined spiritual values of these two religious heritages.[3]

Dear _____,

_____

_____

_____

_____

_____

_____

_____

_____

_____

_____

_____

_____

_____

Questions to Consider

We are asked to promise in the rite of confirmation to "be Christ's disciple, to follow in the way of our Savior, to resist oppression and evil, to show love and justice, and to witness to the work and word of Jesus Christ" as best as we are able.

@ Who are some of the people you turn to as examples of servants or disciples of Christ?

_____

_____

_____

_____

_____

@ What is it about this person(s) that encourages you to be a servant?

_____

_____

_____

_____

_____

@ What value does our culture put on service?

_____

_____

_____

_____

_____

_____

@   How does our culture encourage service? discourage service?

_____

_____

_____

_____

_____

@   How are witness and service connected to the practice of resisting evil?

_____

_____

_____

_____

_____

@   In your own congregation, what ways are persons your age encouraged to serve?

_____

_____

_____

_____

_____

@   What do you wish you could do?

_____

_____

_____

_____

_____

ⓔ   Where do you hear the call to serve in your church?

_____

_____

_____

_____

_____

ⓔ   Where do you hear the call to serve in the world?

_____

_____

_____

_____

_____

ⓔ   How has your own servanthood deepened your faith?

_____

_____

_____

_____

_____

Prayer

Jesus, help me to know how to serve you in the service of others. Help me to make your message of love come alive in the way I live. As I learn to love you more, may I also learn to love the things you love. Amen.

Your Thoughts

_____

_____

_____

_____

_____

_____

_____

_____

_____

_____

_____

_____

_____

_____

_____

_____

_____

1.   *In Mission 1995/96: A Calendar of Prayer for the United Church of Christ* (Cleveland, Ohio: United Church Board for Homeland Ministries and United Church Board for World Ministries, 1995). Used by permission.
2.   *In Mission 1996/97: A Calendar of Prayer for the United Church of Christ* (Cleveland, Ohio: United Church Board for Homeland Ministries and United Church Board for World Ministries, 1996). Used by permission.
3.   Ibid., adapted. Used by permission.

THE SACRAMENTS

19

YOU CALL US INTO YOUR CHURCH . . . TO SHARE IN CHRIST'S BAPTISM AND EAT AT HIS TABLE, TO JOIN HIM IN HIS PASSION AND VICTORY.

—STATEMENT OF FAITH

Themes

- Our covenant with God is established in baptism.
- Our covenant with God is remembered and renewed in Holy Communion.
- The sacraments of baptism and Holy Communion signify God's grace and identify God's people.
- The sacraments of baptism and Holy Communion unite us with Christians in all times and places.

Scriptures

MATTHEW 3:1–17—The account of the baptism of Jesus by John is told.

LUKE 22:1–20—Jesus eats the Last Supper with his disciples.

MATTHEW 28:16–20—Jesus commissions the disciples to baptize and teach.

1 CORINTHIANS 11:23–26—Paul writes about Jesus' meal with the disciples.

Before You Gather

Sacraments are vital in the lives of Christians. They express and nurture the relationship we have with God through Jesus Christ, as an individual and as communities. Our relationship is a covenant. The church has understood covenant as an agreement between God and God's people.

The sacrament of baptism celebrates new life in Jesus Christ. It is the moment when one comes or is brought forward and, with the help and support of the faith community, affirms a covenant with God through Jesus Christ and receives the gift of the Holy Spirit.

Through the sacrament of Holy Communion we renew our covenant with God. The bread and the cup symbolize God's inward and invisible grace at work in us. During communion, we remember Jesus' life, teachings, death, resurrection, and the promise of eternal life. Communion celebrates the gift God gives us in Jesus and celebrates the new covenant we have together in Christ Jesus. When the sacraments are celebrated in worship, they join us together as a group of believers and remind us of the coming of the reign of God.

The sacraments are central to Christian identity. They have been celebrated, in various forms, since the beginning of Christianity. They have been, and are, celebrated in just about every nation on earth. Long after each of us is gone, Christians the world over will still be establishing their covenant with God through baptism and remembering and renewing it through communion.

Baptism Is . . .

Baptism is God's act of grace that expresses God's love, claim, and covenant with a particular individual in the church and incorporates her or him into Christ and the church. Through baptism we are united to Jesus Christ and given part in

Christ's ministry of reconciliation. It is the visible sign of an invisible event: the reconciliation of people to God. It shows the death of self and the rising to a life of obedience and praise. It shows also the pouring out of the Holy Spirit on those whom God has chosen. In baptism, God works in us the power of forgiveness, the renewal of the Spirit, and the knowledge of the call to be God's people always.

Water is an essential element of baptism. Baptism recalls the entire history of God's covenantal action through water. Read the prayer from the "Order for Baptism" from the *United Church of Christ Book of Worship*. Notice how many times the image of water is recalled.

We thank you, God, for the gift of creation called forth by your saving Word. Before the world had shape and form, your Spirit moved over the waters. Out of the waters of the deep, you formed the firmament and brought forth the earth to sustain all life.

In the time of Noah, you washed the earth with the waters of the flood, and your ark of salvation bore a new beginning.

In the time of Moses, your people Israel passed through the Red Sea waters from slavery to freedom and crossed the flowing Jordan to enter the promised land.

In the fullness of time, you sent Jesus Christ, who was nurtured in the water of Mary's womb.

Jesus was baptized by John in the water of the Jordan, became living water to a woman at the Samaritan well, washed the feet of the disciples, and sent them forth to baptize all the nations by water and the Holy Spirit. (The water may be visibly poured.) *Bless by your Holy Spirit, gracious God, this water. By your Holy Spirit save those who confess the name of Jesus Christ that sin may have no power over them. Create new life in all baptized this day that they may rise in Christ. Glory to you, eternal God, the one who was, and is, and shall always be, world without end. Amen.*[1]

Questions of the Candidates

For parents [or guardians] and sponsors of infants and young children:

- Do you desire to have your children baptized into the faith and family of Jesus Christ?

- Will you encourage these children to renounce the powers of evil and to receive the freedom of new life in Christ?

- Will you teach these children that they may be led to profess Jesus Christ as Lord and Savior?

- Do you promise, by the grace of God, to be Christ's disciples, to follow in the way of our Savior, to resist oppression and evil, to show love and justice, and to witness to the work and word of Jesus Christ as best you are able?

- Do you promise, according to the grace given you, to grow with these children in the Christian faith, to help these children to be faithful members of the church of Jesus Christ, by celebrating Christ's presence, by furthering Christ's mission in all the world, and by offering the nurture of the Christian church so that they may affirm their baptism?[2]

These questions may be used when the candidates are able to speak for themselves:

ℰ   Do you desire to be baptized into the faith and family of Jesus Christ?

ℰ   Do you renounce the powers of evil and desire the freedom of new life in Christ?

ℰ   Do you profess Jesus Christ as Lord and Savior?

ℰ   Do you promise, by the grace of God, to be Christ's disciple, to follow in the way of our Savior, to resist oppression and evil, to show love and justice, and to witness to the work and word of Jesus Christ as best you are able?

ℰ   Do you promise, according to the grace given you, to grow in the Christian faith and to be a faithful member of the church of Jesus Christ, celebrating Christ's presence and furthering Christ's mission in all the world?[3]

Baptism is a sacrament that needs to occur only once in a person's life. This "once-for-all-time" quality is because in baptism, God's action of grace is for all time. But there are many ways we can recall the grace and power of our baptism. Some congregations have a time in worship during the year for members to renew the vows made at their baptism. Here's another creative way. The next time you take a shower or a walk in the rain, imagine that the water is God's love and care pouring over you. As the water falls over you, think of any mistakes you've made or things you're sorry you did. Think of the water as giving you new life and imagine that every place that the water touches you is full of God's love and life.

Holy Communion Is . . .

Holy Communion is God's act of grace in which the community takes in Christ
and is empowered by God's Spirit. It recalls the entire history and hope of
God's people who are fed and celebrates God's liberating activity in the world.
At Holy Communion, the breaking of the bread and the pouring of the cup are
symbolic actions that have important meanings. The wheat that is gathered to
make the one loaf and the grapes that are pressed to make one cup remind us
that we are one in the body of Christ. The breaking and the pouring also
remind us of the costliness of Christ's gift of love and life and the discipleship
to which we are all called.[4]

COMMUNION PRAYER

*Holy God, we praise and bless you for creation and the gift of life and for your
abiding love which brings us close to you, the source of all blessing. We thank you
for revealing your will for us in the giving of the law and in the preaching of the
prophets.*

*We thank you especially that in the fullness of time you sent Jesus, born of Mary,
to live in our midst, to share in our suffering, and to accept the pain of death at the
hands of those whom Jesus loved.*

*We rejoice that in a perfect victory over the grave you raised Christ with power to
become sovereign in your realm.*

*We celebrate the coming of the Holy Spirit to gather your church by which your
work may be done in the world and through which we share the gift of eternal life.*

With the faithful in every place and time, we praise with joy your holy name: Holy, holy, holy God of love and majesty, the whole universe speaks of your glory, O God Most High.

We remember that on the night of betrayal and desertion, Jesus took bread, gave you thanks, broke the bread, and gave it to the disciples, saying: "This is my body which is broken for you. Do this in remembrance of me."

In the same way, Jesus also took the cup, after supper, saying: "This cup is the new covenant in my blood. Do this, as often as you drink it, in remembrance of me."

Consecrate, therefore, by your Holy Spirit, these gifts of bread and wine, and bless us that as we receive them at this table, we may offer you our faith and praise, we may be united with Christ and with one another, and we may continue faithful in all things.

In the strength Christ gives us, we offer ourselves to you, eternal God, and give thanks that you have called us to serve you. Amen.[5]

BREAKING BREAD AND POURING CUP

While taking the bread and breaking it: Through the broken bread we participate in the body of Christ.

While pouring the wine and raising the cup: Through the cup of blessing we participate in the new life Christ gives.[6]

SHARING THE ELEMENTS

While giving the bread: Eat this, for it is the body of Christ, broken for you.

While giving the cup: Drink this, for it is the blood of Christ, shed for you.[7]

PRAYER OF THANKSGIVING

We thank you, God, for inviting us to this table where we have known the presence of Christ and have received all Christ's gifts. Strengthen our faith, increase our love for one another, and let us show forth your praise in our lives; through Jesus Christ our Savior. Amen.[8]

The next time you eat a meal with other people try to imagine that Christ is there with you. Imagine Christ eating the same food, laughing at the same things, hearing the same conversation. With each bite you take, think about Christ's love for you, how Christ is really there with you, as real as the food and drink at your meal.

Questions to Consider

℮ At baptism, which promises asked of the candidates, parents or guardians, sponsors, and congregation do you think would be the easiest to keep? Why?

_____

_____

_____

_____

℮ At baptism, which promises asked of the candidates, parents or guardians, sponsors, and congregation do you think would be the most difficult to keep? Why?

_____

_____

_____

_____

℮ Communion practices vary throughout the United Church of Christ. Some congregations celebrate communion weekly, some monthly, and some on special holidays,
such as World Communion Sunday, Christmas, Ash Wednesday, Holy Thursday,
Easter, and Pentecost. When does your congregation celebrate communion?

_____

_____

_____

_____

℮ Where does the communion happen in the order of worship?

_____

_____

_____

_____

℮ Who is invited to participate? Why?

_____

_____

_____

_____

℮ How are the bread and cup served? (In the pews or by coming forward; using a
common cup or individual cups; by intinction, where the bread is dipped in the
juice and eaten individually.)

_____

_____

_____

_____

@   Is grape juice or wine or both used?

_____

_____

_____

_____

@   What kind of bread is used? Why?

_____

_____

_____

_____

@   What is the mood in church when Holy Communion is celebrated? Why do you

suppose this is? How is the mood conveyed?

_____

_____

_____

_____

Prayer

Thank you, God, for inviting me to share in Christ's baptism and eat at Christ's table. Amen.

Your Thoughts

_____

_____

_____

_____

_____

_____

_____

_____

_____

_____

_____

_____

_____

_____

_____

_____

_____

1. *United Church of Christ Book of Worship* (New York: Office for Church Life and Leadership, 1986), 141–42. Used by permission.
2. Ibid., 136–37. Used by permission.
3. Ibid., 138–39. Used by permission.
4. Ibid., 32–33. Used by permission.
5. Ibid., 84–86. Used by permission.
6. Ibid., 86. Used by permission.
7. Ibid., 87. Used by permission.
8. Ibid., 88. Used by permission.

What's best in
life comes to
us from
God, not as
a result of
our efforts
or talents,
but by sheer
gift.

GOD'S GIFTS AND OUR RESPONSE

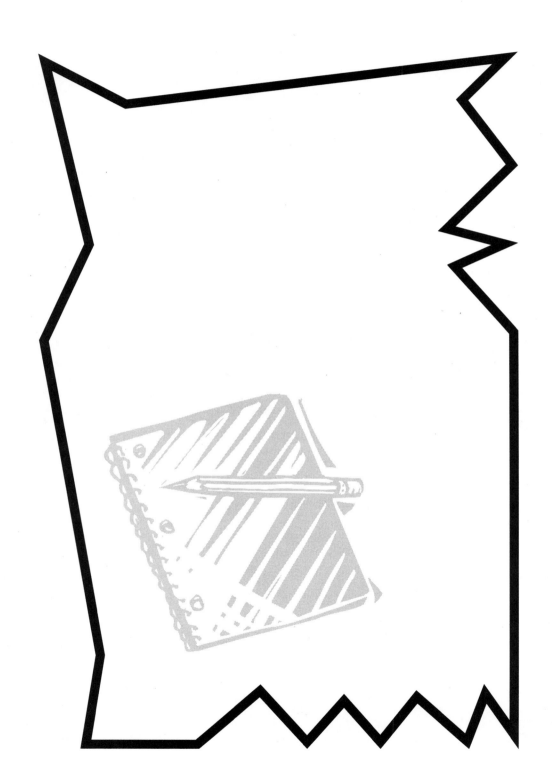

FORGIVENESS AND GRACE **20**

YOU PROMISE TO ALL WHO TRUST YOU FORGIVENESS OF SINS AND FULLNESS OF GRACE.

—STATEMENT OF FAITH

Themes

- Grace abounds and we have much for which to be grateful.
- God's grace is sufficient; God's forgiveness is always available.
- God's grace doesn't prevent suffering; it accompanies the one who suffers.

Scriptures

MATTHEW 20:1–16—Jesus tells the parable of the laborers in the vineyard.

COLOSSIANS 3:12–17—God's chosen ones are to clothe themselves with love, forgive one another, and let Christ's peace rule in their hearts.

Before You Gather

In a world in which "there's no such thing as a free lunch"—a world in which nearly everything desirable must either be earned or paid for—the concept of grace may seem very strange. One of the most wonderful ways in which grace is offered to us is as forgiveness for what we've done wrong. One of the Bible's major themes is that God forgives our sin. God does not hold our mistakes and our hurting of others against us. This is not to say that "anything goes," that whatever we do no matter how mean or insensitive is acceptable in God's sight. It is not.

Sin can be defined as "separation." It is separation from God, others, and our sense of responsible connection to creation. As we confess our sin, as we say the ways in which we have let God, others, and ourselves down, God gives us a new beginning. When we confess our sins, forgiveness, through grace, is offered whether we "deserve" it or not.

Because God offers us grace, we are called to be gracious with others. What makes an act gracious or forgiving in our own interactions with others? If it is done freely and generously, without regard to whether someone has earned or deserved it, it is an act of grace and forgiveness.

The presence of grace (and of God) does *not* mean the absence of suffering. Recognizing the grace that has been given to us does not mean that we will be spared all pain. Being human means that trauma, despair, grief, and failure cannot be evaded. What can be affirmed is that grace is often known most profoundly in the midst of pain or despair.

A Modern Parable

God's special world is like this. The owner of a video store had a number of full-time workers whom she paid pretty well. One year, because the Christmas rush was coming, early in December she hired extra workers for the season. She promised to pay them what was right. A week later, and again two weeks later, she did the same thing. Finally, on the morning of Christmas Eve, anticipating a frenetic day, she did the same thing. "I need you to work in the store too," she said. When that last day before Christmas had finally ended, she called all her workers to her to pay them. First she paid those she had hired that day. She paid them as if they had been there for the entire month. Then she paid those who had come two weeks ago, then those who had started three weeks ago. Each of them also got a full month's wage.

When the full-time workers came, they expected they would receive more. But each of them received what the others had been given. And when they looked at their paychecks, they bad-mouthed their boss, saying, "The last people you hired worked only a day, and you have made them equal to those of us who worked so hard for the whole month."

But the owner said to them, "I'm not doing anything wrong to you. Didn't we agree on your pay? Take what belongs to you and go. I choose to give to the ones I hired today the same as I give to you. Am I not allowed to do what I choose with what belongs to me? Or are you envious because I am generous? So the last will be first, and the first will be last."

Questions to Consider

We have all done things for which we feel truly sorry and for which we need to ask for forgiveness.

@   What would you like to ask God's forgiveness for?

On three small pieces of paper write down some things for which you seek forgiveness. Then read each one and pray, "God, please forgive me." Each time you pray, tear the paper into small pieces and throw it away. After each one pray, "Thank you, God, for forgiving me. Help me to make a fresh start." After this, sing, hum, or say the first verse of the hymn "Amazing Grace," found on page 228.

@ Who do you need to forgive?

Think about someone you're angry with or who may have hurt you. Close your eyes
and say to God, "God, help me know how to forgive and give me the strength
to do it." Keep still for a few minutes and see how you feel. In your journal draw
pictures of how you feel. It may help to write the person a letter that you will
not send, saying how you feel and why.

If you find it difficult to forgive, you may want to talk to a trusted adult, like a pastor, counselor, or teacher who can help you understand your anger or hurt and
what to do about it.

@   Who do you need to ask forgiveness of?

Now think about someone who is angry with you or who you have hurt. Close your
    eyes and say to God, "God, help me to know how to ask for forgiveness for the
    wrong I have done." Keep still for a few minutes and see how you feel. In your
    journal draw pictures of how you feel. It may help to write the person a letter
    that you will not send, saying how you feel and why.
Ask God for forgiveness. If it is appropriate, go to the person and ask for forgive-
    ness as well.

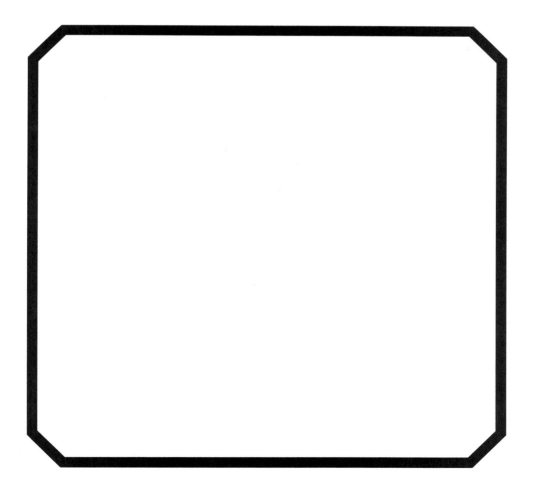

A Worship Litany

One: *Let us pray. O God, we give thanks today for your incredible blessings,*

All: *For the bounties of earth and sky,*

One: *For the great generosity of family, friends, teachers, and church members,*

All: *For the privileges that we enjoy.*

One: *We give thanks, as well, for the power of forgiveness.*

All: *Open our eyes and hearts, so that we may see how much comes to us by sheer gift.*

One: *And help us to live always as grateful people. Amen.*

All: *Amen.*

Prayer

Sometimes it is easier to keep a grudge than to forgive. As you forgive me the wrong things I do, O God, may I learn to forgive others. May I also learn to accept the forgiveness of others I have wronged. Help me to trust in your grace and the power of forgiveness. Amen.

Your Thoughts

_____

_____

_____

_____

_____

_____

_____

_____

_____

_____

_____

_____

_____

_____

_____

_____

_____

_____

JUSTICE AND PEACE

YOU PROMISE TO ALL WHO TRUST YOU . . . COURAGE IN THE STRUGGLE FOR JUSTICE AND PEACE, YOUR PRESENCE IN TRIAL AND REJOICING.

—STATEMENT OF FAITH

Themes

- God is a God of justice and peace.
- God has a special regard for the poor and the oppressed and requires that we show this same regard for them.
- God is present in times of trial and times of joy.

Scriptures

ISAIAH 58:6–12—God opposes injustice and cares for those in need.

PHILIPPIANS 4:4–7—The faithful are called to rejoice in God.

Before You Gather

God's justice is about the rights of individuals and communities in need. God's peace is about the wholeness or well-being of persons and groups. The struggle for justice and peace requires us to place our trust and courage in a God who promises to be with us, through the presence of the Spirit, in moments of deep joy and in moments of great difficulty.

God supports action that shows regard for the poor and the oppressed. God's demand for acts of justice and peace are so significant that other responses we may have are of little or no value without paying attention to those in need.

The struggle for justice and peace requires us to anchor our trust and courage on God, who promises to be with us, no matter what may happen to us. The words from Philippians 4:7 assure us that "the peace of God, which surpasses all understanding, will guard your hearts and minds in Christ Jesus."

Questions to Consider

Find a place you can be alone with yourself and God. Get comfortable and relaxed. Think about the volunteer or community service work you have done as part of this faith formation process or any volunteer or community service work you've done at another time. If you have not done volunteer work, think about times you have helped others.

Try to remember what you were thinking and feeling before you began the experience.

@ Were you anxious? Did you think you would be bored? excited? Would it be fun? hard?

@ What did you think it was going to be like?

Now think about the experience itself.

@ Who did you work with? What were they like? Did you learn anything about them? Did you learn anything about yourself?

@ What were you feeling while you were working? Did it match your expectations? How was it different?

@ Did you feel you were doing God's will to seek justice and peace?

Write or draw about your experience and reflections.

Liz's Story

One summer evening a friend and I had just come out of a coffee shop and stopped to hear this guy sing and play guitar on the street. It was obvious that he was homeless; he seemed to have all his belongings in a backpack. Nearby a large group of other people who were homeless were laying out blankets or very ratty-looking sleeping bags, getting ready for the night. They too were enjoying the guitar player's music. We stood there for about five minutes and decided to sit on the sidewalk to keep listening.

One of the homeless people sitting on a blanket turned to us and asked if we wanted to share her blanket. She said it wasn't much, but it was softer than the sidewalk. We were a little timid, but we accepted her invitation. Then the people began pulling out bags of food; most of it looked like it had been retrieved from Dumpsters and garbage cans. They shared with one another until it seemed everyone was fed; they even offered some to us, even though I'm sure we looked like well-fed students. I learned a lot that night about true Christian love and sharing. I learned that if people who have nothing can share and help each other then I can too.

Population of the World

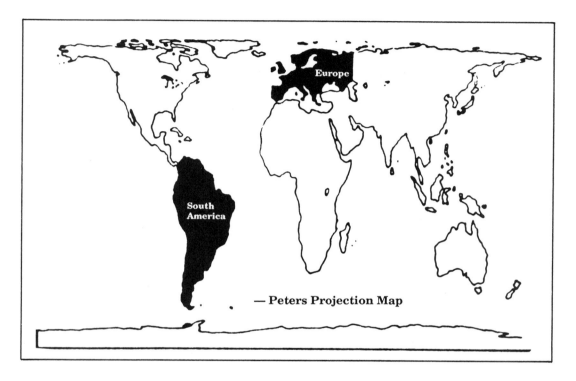

South America

Europe

— Peters Projection Map

Source: Reprinted, by permission of the publisher, from *Make a World of Difference: Creative Activities for Global Learning* (Cincinnati: Office of Global Education, National Council of Churches in Christ, 1989), 57.

CONTINENT	ESTIMATED POPULATION (%)	ACTUAL POPULATION (%)
Africa	_____	_____
Asia	_____	_____
Europe	_____	_____
North America	_____	_____
South America	_____	_____

Final Phrases in the Psalms

What words or phrases in the Psalms match these ideas from the Statement of
Faith?

@   [God] promises to all who trust [God] . . .

_____

_____

_____

_____

_____

_____

@   courage in the struggle for justice and peace,

_____

_____

_____

_____

_____

_____

@   [God's] presence in trial and rejoicing.

_____

_____

_____

_____

_____

_____

Write or Draw Your Own Psalm

Prayer

God of all creation, you call us to rejoice in all things, trusting in you to show us the way of justice and peace. Sometimes this is difficult. Justice and peace are not always welcome. Help me to know that you are with me when I work for justice and peace. Help me to remember that your peace surpasses all understanding. Amen.

Your Thoughts

ETERNAL LIFE

YOU PROMISE TO ALL WHO TRUST YOU . . . ETERNAL LIFE IN YOUR REALM WHICH HAS NO END.

—STATEMENT OF FAITH

Themes

@ Eternal life is a gift from God.

@ Eternal life is given to believers now, but its fullness is known after we die.

Scriptures

JOHN 17:1–3—Eternal life is knowing God.

JOHN 5:24–29—Through Christ the coming age of God's reign is now here.

REVELATION 4:1–6—A vision of heaven is described.

ROMANS 8:31–39—Nothing can separate us from the love of God.

Before You Gather

Eternal life is a gift from God. Eternal life is not something that we can manufacture or earn. It can only be received as a gift. Eternal life can't be managed or controlled. It is the result of God's grace rather than our abilities. It is granted by God alone.

It is available both in the life to come and in this life. Eternal life is not just something given to us once our bodies give out. It is something available to us now, not just in some distant future, but now right now, by faith in Jesus Christ. We are in God's care both now and forevermore. We can trust that God cares for us and that wherever we go we can find God's love. To have faith in and know God is to receive and accept this unearned grace.

There is a second part to what it means to have faith in and know God. Faith both receives divine care and spreads it. If you want to know eternal life, give yourself not just to friends and family, but to all creation.

Journal Your Thoughts about Heaven

Read the story. Then write words, phrases, feelings or draw images that you associate with the idea of heaven.

RICARDO'S STORY

The first year I was a counselor at church camp there was a dance at the end of the week. The music started and I was suddenly transported back to my first year in high school at my first school dance. It was awful. No one really danced except the people who were already in couples, and they only danced the slow dances. The rest of us just stood around wanting to dance, but none of us were brave enough to do it. My mind came back to the present and I realized that this dance at camp was different.

People didn't wait to be asked and they didn't dance in couples. Everyone started dancing in big circles and cheering each other on. People who probably wouldn't even have talked to each other at school were dancing next to each other. Country western fans were teaching head bangers how to two-step and rockers were showing rappers how to slam dance so they wouldn't get hurt. It was amazing. I remember thinking that if heaven is the place where everyone lives in peace and harmony, then this must be what Jesus talked about when he said, "The Reign of God is at hand!" God's love and acceptance poured down on us that night and we shared it with each other.

@ What words, phrases, feelings, or images do you associate with the idea of heaven?

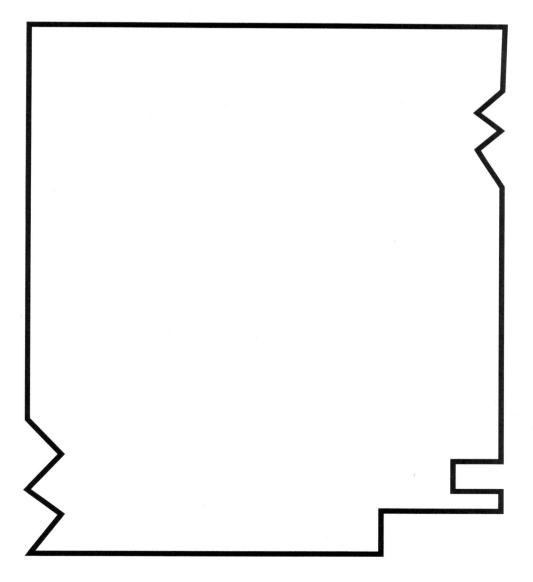

Read the lyrics to Eric Clapton's song "Tears in Heaven." He wrote this song after his young son died accidentally.

TEARS IN HEAVEN

Would you know my name
    if I saw you in heaven?
Would it be the same
    if I saw you in heaven?

I must be strong
    and carry on
'cause I know I don't belong
    here in heaven.

Would you hold my hand
    if I saw you in heaven?
Would you help me stand
    if I saw you in heaven?
I'll find my way
    through night and day
'cause I know I just can't stay
    here in heaven.

Time can bring you down,
    time can bend your knees.
Time can break your heart,
    have you beggin' please, beggin'
    please.

Beyond the door
    there's peace, I'm sure.
And I know there'll be
    no more tears in heaven.

Would you know my name
    if I saw you in heaven?
Would you be the same
    if I saw you in heaven?

I must be strong
    and carry on
'cause I know
    I don't belong here in heaven,
'cause I know
    I don't belong here in heaven.

Write additional words, phrases, feelings, or images you associate with the idea of heaven.

Questions to Consider

One of Christianity's fundamental convictions is that God cares for us after we die—that death is in no way the end of our connection to God. God gives us eternal life, and that gift does not stop with physical death.

℮ What do you imagine that kind of care from God is like?

_____

_____

℮ How is that kind of care expressed by God to us here and now?

_____

_____

℮ How would you describe "heaven on earth"?

_____

_____

℮ What are the things you can do for and with others to help them experience heaven now? listen to music that gives you a sense of joy and peace? work to change an unjust situation like poverty or racism? walk in a beautiful place? enjoy the company of good and loving friends? choose something you can do for and with another person or other part of creation?

_____

_____

_____

_____

Prayer

O God, as I approach the time of choosing to be committed to you, I know that you have already chosen me! In knowing you and making you known to others, I will see and share what is eternal. Help me trust that in this life and even in death, you are always with me. Amen.

Your Thoughts

_____

_____

_____

_____

_____

_____

_____

_____

_____

_____

_____

_____

_____

_____

_____

_____

_____

_____

_____

_____

THE FAITH JOURNEY

CONTINUES

What Do I Think?

Reflect on these questions:

◉ In what ways does my faith in Jesus Christ influence and shape my life?

_____

_____

_____

◉ How will my faith shape my future?

_____

_____

_____

The Call of Jeremiah

The Bible is full of stories of God calling people—Abraham and Sarah, Moses,
   Aaron and Miriam, Ruth, Esther, Samuel, Elizabeth, Mary, Paul, Timothy, and
   many others—to important tasks of love, justice, and mission. But one story
   can be especially meaningful for you. It is the story of the call of Jeremiah.
   When God called Jeremiah to become a prophet, Jeremiah was only fourteen
   or fifteen years old. The story of the call is found in Jeremiah 1:4–10.

QUESTIONS TO CONSIDER

@ How do you think Jeremiah felt when he was asked to become one of God's prophets?

@ How do you think you would feel?

@ How do you think God calls people today?

@ How do you think one experiences God's call?

@ Who are some people today whom God has called?

@ What are some ways people show that they have answered God's call?

Questions of the Candidates[1]

@ Do you desire to affirm your baptism/be baptized into the faith and family of Jesus Christ?

@ Do you renounce the power of evil and desire the freedom of new life in Christ?

@ Do you profess Jesus Christ as Lord and Savior?

@ Do you promise, by the grace of God, to be Christ's disciple, to follow in the way of our Savior, to resist oppression and evil, to show love and justice, and to witness to the work and word of Jesus Christ as best you are able?

@ Do you promise, according to the grace given you, to grow in the Christian faith and to be a faithful member of the church of Jesus Christ, celebrating Christ's presence and furthering Christ's mission in all the world?

Write a Prayer

Write a short prayer. It may contain honest wishes, honest doubts, and honest fears. You can use the prayers below as models for your prayer, if you wish.

Lord God, I have no idea where I am going. / I do not see the road ahead of me, / I cannot know for certain where it will end. / Nor do I really know myself, / and the fact that I think that I am following your will / does not mean that I am actually doing so. / I believe that the desire to please you does in fact please you. / I hope that I have that desire in all that I am doing. / I hope that I will never do anything apart from that desire. / I know that if I do this you will lead me by the right road / though I may know nothing about it. / Therefore will I trust you always / though I may seem lost. . . . / I will not fear, / for you are ever with me, / and will never leave me . . . alone.

—*Thomas Merton*[2]

Speak God, for your servant hears. / Grant us ears to hear, / eyes to see, / wills to obey, / hearts to love; / then declare what you will, / reveal what you will, command what you will, / demand what you will. Amen.

—*Christina G. Rossetti*[3]

God be in my head, and in my understanding;
God be in my eyes, and in my looking;
God be in my mouth, and in my speaking;
God be in my heart, and in my thinking;
God be at my end, and at my departing.

—*Old Sarum Primer*[4]

YOUR PRAYER

_____
_____
_____
_____
_____
_____
_____
_____
_____
_____
_____
_____
_____
_____
_____
_____
_____
_____
_____
_____
_____
_____
_____
_____
_____
_____

Call to Worship[5]

One: *Everything as it moves, now and then, here and there, makes pauses.*

All: *The bird as it flies stops on one place to make its nest, and in another to rest in its flight.*

One: *In the same way, God has paused as well.*

All: *The sun, which is so bright and beautiful, is one place where God has paused.*

One: *The moon, the stars, the winds; God has been with them, too.*

All: *The trees, the animals, are all places where God has stopped, leaving the touch of the Holy in all these things.*

One: *We, too, have had God pause in us. We too have the Holy touch in our being.*

All: *Let us now pause ourselves, and listen for the voice of God on our hearts.*

—Teachings of the Lakota

Your Thoughts

_____

_____

_____

_____

_____

_____

_____

_____

_____

_____

_____

_____

_____

_____

_____

_____

_____

_____

_____

_____

_____

_____

1. *United Church of Christ Book of Worship* (New York: United Church of Christ Office of Church Life and Leadership, 1986), 149. Used by permission.
2. Adapted from Mark Link, *Breakway: Twenty-eight Steps to a More Prayerful Life* (Allen, Tex.: Argus Communications, 1980), 51.
3. Adapted from George Appleton, ed., *The Oxford Book of Prayer* (London: Oxford University Press, 1985), 91.
4. Ibid., 90.
5. Juanita J. Helphrey, comp., *Worship Resources* (Minneapolis: United Church of Christ Council for American Indian Ministries, 1991), 28. Copyright 1991, United Church of Christ Council for American Indian Ministries. Used by permission.

Gathered Here

Text and Music: Phil Porter, 1990

Gath-ered here in the mys-tery of this hour, gath-ered here in one strong

bod - y, gath-ered here in the strug-gle and the power, Spir - it draw near.

This chant may be sung as a round.

Great Work Has God Begun in You

Carol Birkland, 1995

Tune: VERBUM DEI L.M.
William P. Rowan, 1993
Alternate tune: PUER NOBIS NASCITUR

1 Great work has God be - gun in you, so let the Spir - it
2 In love, God calls you to this day, and gives you strength, these
3 A - round God's ta - ble cel - e - brate the end of bond - age,
4 Great work has God be - gun in you; take on God's love in

fol - low through; The mark of Christ up - on your brow, bap -
vows to say; Take up the faith that you were shown, and
sin, and hate: A feast of love and vic - to - ry, the
all you do, And may that love in you in - crease—now,

tis - mal touch re - mem - ber now.
grow, as - sured you are God's own.
gift of Christ who sets us free.
with God's bless - ing, go in peace.

Bring Many Names

Brian Wren, 1989

Tune: WESTCHASE 9.10.11.9.
Carlton R. Young, 1989

1 Bring man- y names, beau - ti - ful and good, cel - e- brate, in
2 Strong moth- er God, work- ing night and day, plan- ning all the
3 Warm fa - ther God, hug- ging ev - ery child, feel- ing all the
4 Old, ach- ing God, grey with end- less care, calm - ly pierc- ing

par - a - ble and sto- ry, ho - li - ness in glo- ry, liv- ing, lov- ing God.
won- ders of cre - a - tion, set- ting each e - qua- tion, gen - i - us at play:
strains of hu- man liv- ing, car- ing and for- giv- ing till we're rec- on- ciled:
e - vil's new dis- guis- es, glad of good sur- pris- es, wis- er than de- spair:

1–5   6

Hail   and Ho- san- na! bring man- y names!   great, liv- ing God!
Hail   and Ho- san- na, strong moth- er God!
Hail   and Ho- san- na, warm   fa- ther God!
Hail   and Ho- san- na, old,   ach- ing God!

5   Young, grow-ing God, ea-ger,
          on the move,
     say-ing no to false-hood and
          un-kind-ness,
             cry-ing out for jus-tice,
             giv-ing all you have:
     Hail and Ho-san-na,
     young, grow-ing God!

6   Great, liv-ing God, nev-er ful-ly known,
          joy-ful dark-ness far be-yond our see-ing,
             clo-ser yet than breath-ing,
             ev-er-last-ing home:
     Hail and Ho-san-na,
     great, liv-ing God!

I Thank You, Jesus

Words and music: Kenneth Morris, 1948; alt.

Arr. by Joyce Finch Johnson, 1992

brought me from a might-y, a might-y long way (a might-y long way).
brought me from a might-y, a might-y long way (a might-y long way).

For All the Saints

William W. How, 1864; alt.

Tune: SINE NOMINE 10.10.10.4.
Ralph Vaughan Williams, 1906

1 For all the saints   who from their la-bors rest,   who to the
2 You were the rock,   their ref-uge, and their might: you, Christ, the
3 Still may your peo-ple, faith-ful, true, and bold,   live as the
4 Ringed by this cloud   of wit-ness-es di-vine,   we fee-bly
5 And when the strife   is fierce, the war-fare long,   steals on the

world their stead-fast faith con-fessed,   your name, O Je-sus,
hope that put their fears to flight;   'mid gloom and doubt, you
saints who no-bly fought of old,   and share with them a
strug-gle, they in glo-ry shine;   yet in your love our
ear the dis-tant tri-umph song,   then hearts are brave a-

be for - ev - er blessed.
were their one true light.
glo - rious crown of gold. Al - le - lu - ia! Al - le - lu - ia!
faith - ful lives en - twine.
gain, and faith grows strong.

Let Us Break Bread Together

African American spiritual

Tune: LET US BREAK BREAD
10.10. with refrain
Harm. David Hurd, 1983

1 Let us break bread to-geth-er on our knees;
*2 Let us drink wine to-geth-er on our knees;
3 Let us praise God to-geth-er on our knees;

let us break bread to-geth-er on our knees.
let us drink wine to-geth-er on our knees.
let us praise God to-geth-er on our knees.

* "Share the cup" *may be substituted for* "drink wine."

When I fall on my knees, with my face to the ris-ing sun,

My God, have mer-cy on me.

Spirit of the Living God

Daniel Iverson, 1926

Tune: IVERSON 7.5.7.5.8.7.5.
Daniel Iverson, 1926

Nada te Turbe
(Nothing Can Trouble)

Text: The Taizé Community, 1991

Music: Jacques Berthier, 1991

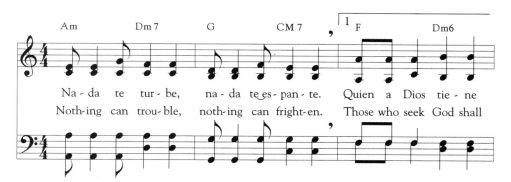

We Are Your People

Brian Wren, 1973; rev. 1993

Tune: WHITFIELD Irr.
John W. Wilson, 1975

Unison

1 We are your peo - ple: Spir - it of grace,
2 Joined in com - mu - ni - ty, trea - sured and fed,
3 Rich in di - ver - si - ty, help us to live
4 Glad of tra - di - tion, help us to see

you dare to make us Christ to our neigh - bors
may we dis - cov - er gifts in each oth - er,
clos - er than neigh - bors, o - pen to strang - ers,
in all life's chang - ing, where Christ is lead - ing,

1 & 6   *Last time, end*   **2–5**

of ev - ery cul - ture and place.
will - ing to lead and be led.
a - ble to clash and for - give.
where our best ef - forts should be.

5 Give, as we ven-ture
  jus-tice and care
    (peace-ful, in-sist-ing,
    risk-ing, re-sist-ing),
  wis-dom to know when and where.

6 Spir-it, u-nite us,
  make us, by grace,
    will-ing and read-y,
    Christ's liv-ing bod-y,
  lov-ing the whole hu-man race.

Be Still

Ps. 46:10

Music: Anon.

Be still and know that I am God. Be still and know that

I am God. Be still and know that I am God.

Tú Has Venido a la Orilla
(You Have Come Down to the Lakeshore)

Cesáreo Gabaraín, 1979; alt.
Transl. Madeleine Forell Marshall, 1989; alt.

Tune: PESCADOR DE HOMBRES
8.10.10. with refrain
Cesáreo Gabaraín, 1979
Harm. Skinner Chávez-Melo, 1987

(continued on next page)

3 Tú ne-ce-si-tas mis ma-nos,
   mi can-san-cio que a o-tros des-can-se,
   a-mor que quie-ra se-guir a-man-do.
   Estribillo

4 Tú, Pes-ca-dor de o-tros ma-res,
   an-sia e-ter-na de al-mas que es-pe-ran.
   A-mi-go bue-no, que a-sí me lla-mas.
   Estribillo

3 You need my hands, my ex-haus-tion,
   work-ing love for the rest of the
        wea-ry—
   A love that's will-ing to go on lov-ing.
   Refrain

4 You who have fished oth-er wa-ters;
   you, the long-ing of souls that are
        yearn-ing:
   As lov-ing Friend, you have come
        to call me.
   Refrain

Amazing Grace, How Sweet the Sound
(Onuniyan tehanl waun)

St. 1–4, John Newton, 1779; alt.
St. 5, *A Collection of Sacred Ballads*, 1790
Lakota trans. Stephen W. Holmes, 1987

Tune: AMAZING GRACE C.M.
(NEW BRITAIN)
Columbia Harmony, Cincinnati, 1829
Arr. Edwin O. Excell, 1900

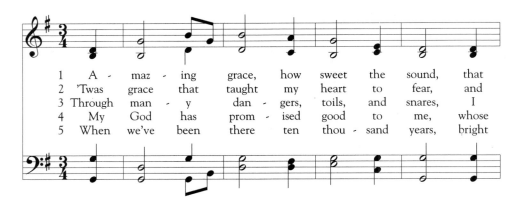

1 A - maz - ing   grace,   how sweet the   sound,   that
2 'Twas grace   that   taught   my   heart   to   fear,   and
3 Through man - y   dan - gers,   toils, and   snares,   I
4 My   God   has prom - ised good   to   me,   whose
5 When we've been there   ten thou - sand years, bright

saved a wretch like me! I once was lost, but
grace my fears re - lieved; How pre - cious did that
have al - read - y come; 'Tis grace has brought me
word my hope se - cures; God will my shield and
shin - ing as the sun, We've no less days to

now am found, was blind but now I see.
grace ap - pear the hour I first be - lieved!
safe thus far, and grace will lead me home.
por - tion be as long as life en - dures.
sing God's praise than when we'd first be - gun.

1 O-nu-ni-yan te-hanl wa-un,
   Ma-shi-cha tke wa-ni,
  Wo-wash-te kin i-ye-wa-ye,
   wi-cho-ni wan-bla-ke.

2 Wo-wash-te he chan-te ma-hel,
   wash-ag-ma-ya-yin kte,
  Wo-wi cha-ke kin un le-hanl,
   o-a-pe kin wan-na.

3 O-ta kig-le te-ke wan el,
   eg-na i-ma-cha-ge,
  Wo-wash-te kin hel ma-wa-ni,
   Wash-te o-ma-ju-la.

4 O-to-ka-he-ya chi-ya-tan,
   o-hin-ni-yan ya-un,
  Wa-kan-tan-ka wo-wi-tan kin,
   yu-ha ma-wa-ni kte.

5 Wa-kan-tan-ka ya-tan un-we,
   Wa-kan-tan-ka ya-tan,
  Wa-kan-tan-ka ya-tan un-we,
   wa-kan-tan-ka a-men.

Called as Partners in Christ's Service

Jane Parker Huber, 1981

Tune: BEECHER 8.7.8.7.D.
John Zundel, 1855

1 Called as part-ners in Christ's ser-vice, called to min-is-tries of grace,
2 Christ's ex-am-ple, Christ's in-spir-ing, Christ's clear call to work and worth,
3 Thus new pat-terns for Christ's mis-sion, in a small or glob-al sense,
4 So God grant us for to-mor-row ways to or-der hu-man life

We re-spond with deep com-mit-ment fresh new lines of faith to trace.
Let us fol-low, nev-er fal-tering, rec-on-cil-ing folk on earth.
Help us bear each oth-er's bur-dens, break-ing down each wall or fence.
That sur-round each per-son's sor-row with a calm that con-quers strife.

May we learn the art of shar-ing, side by side and friend with friend,
Men and wom-en, rich-er, poor-er, all God's peo-ple, young and old,
Words of com-fort, words of vi-sion, words of chal-lenge, said with care,
Make us part-ners in our liv-ing, our com-pas-sion to in-crease,

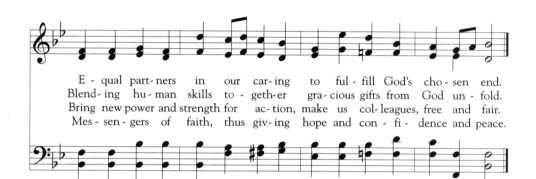

E - qual part-ners in our car-ing to ful - fill God's cho - sen end.
Blend- ing hu - man skills to - geth-er gra - cious gifts from God un - fold.
Bring new power and strength for ac- tion, make us col- leagues, free and fair.
Mes - sen - gers of faith, thus giv- ing hope and con - fi - dence and peace.

Wakantanka Taku Nitawa
(Many and Great, O God, Are Your Works)

Dakota hymn, Joseph R. Renville, 1842
Paraphr. by R. Philip Frazier, 1929; alt.

Tune: LACQUIPARLE 9.6.9.9.9.6.
Native American melody (Dakota)
Adapt. Joseph R. Renville, 1842
Harm. James R. Murray, 1877

Optional hand-drum rhythm:

1 Wa - kan - tan - ka   ta - ku   ni - ta - wa   tan - ka - ya
2 Wo - eh - da - ku   ni - ta - wa kin   he   mi - na - gi
1 Man - y   and   great,   O   God,   are your works,   Mak - er   of
2 Grant un - to   us   com - mu - nion with   you,   O   star a -

qa   o - ta;   Ma - hpi - ya   kin   e - ya - hna - ke   ca,
kin   qu   wo;   Ma - hpi - ya   kin   i - wan - kam ya - ti,
earth   and   sky;   Your   hands have   set   the   heav - ens with   stars,
bid - ing   One;   Come   un - to   us   and   dwell   with   us:

ma - ka   kin   he   du - o - wan - ca,   Mni - o - wan -
wi - co - wa - šte   yu - ha   nan - ka,   Wi - co - ni
your   fin - gers   spread   the   moun - tains and   plains.   Lo,   at   your
with   you   are   found   the   gifts   of   life.   Bless   us   with

ca śbe - ya wan - ke cin, he - na o - ya - ki - hi.
kin he ma - ya - qu nun, o - wi - han - ke wa - nin.
word the wa - ters were formed; deep seas o - bey your voice.
life that has no end, e - ter - nal life with you.

Creeds and Statements of Faith

APOSTLES' CREED

I believe in God, the Father almighty,

    creator of heaven and earth.

I believe in Jesus Christ, God's only Son, our Lord,

    who was conceived by the Holy Spirit,

    born of the Virgin Mary,

    suffered under Pontius Pilate,

    was crucified, died and was buried;

    he descended to the dead.

On the third day he rose again;

    he ascended into heaven,

    he is seated at the right hand of the Father,

    and he will come to judge the living and the dead.

I believe in the Holy Spirit,

    the holy catholic Church,

    the communion of the saints,

    the forgiveness of sins,

    the resurrection of the body,

    and the life everlasting. Amen.

—English Language Liturgical Consultation[1]

UNITED CHURCH OF CHRIST STATEMENT OF FAITH IN THE FORM OF A DOXOLOGY

We believe in you, O God, Eternal Spirit,

God of our Savior Jesus Christ and our God,

and to your deeds we testify:

    You call the worlds into being,

create persons in your own image,

and set before each one the ways of life and death.

You seek in holy love to save all people from aimlessness and sin.

You judge people and nations by your righteous will declared through prophets and apostles.

In Jesus Christ, the man of Nazareth, our crucified and risen Savior,

you have come to us

and shared our common lot,

conquering sin and death

and reconciling the world to yourself.

You bestow upon us your Holy Spirit,

creating and renewing the church of Jesus Christ,

binding in covenant faithful people of all ages, tongues, and races.

You call us into your church

to accept the cost and joy of discipleship,

to be your servants in the service of others,

to proclaim the gospel to all the world and resist the powers of evil,

to share in Christ's baptism and eat at his table,

to join him in his passion and victory.

You promise to all who trust you

forgiveness of sins and fullness of grace,

courage in the struggle for justice and peace,

your presence in trial and rejoicing,

and eternal life in your realm which has no end.

Blessing and honor, glory and power be unto you. Amen.[2]

A Service of Dedication for Confirmands, Leaders, and Mentors[3]

Here is a service of dedication that can be used at the beginning of a faith formation program before the opening retreat is held.

THE JOURNEY OF FAITH

Pastor (or another leader): All Christians are on a journey. It is a journey to a place where we seek to find meaning in life, to that place where we come to know God. It is a journey away from the place where we think of ourselves first, to the place where we can offer ourselves to others. All of us are on this journey for the duration of our lives. Ours is a journey of learning—in which we seek to learn more about God and how to please God. Ours is a journey of growing—in which we seek to mature in those ways we may serve God more faithfully.

These young people come before us today because they have come to a significant point in their own journeys. They are about to engage in an intentional faith formation process together, with the hope that, at its conclusion, they may join us in publicly affirming the Christian faith into which we have been baptized.

These adults from our congregation have agreed to be present with the youth as guides [and mentors] for the length of this process. As such, they will share with them their own faith, learning along with them.

But faith formation requires the support of the entire community of faith. Therefore, as these people take their next steps in faith, they need our support, encouragement, and prayers. I therefore ask each of you to express your commitment to the next segment of the faith journey these young people are about to make.

Pastor (addressing the confirmands): Do you desire to join with one another and with your leaders [and mentors] to journey together in the Christian faith? Do you wish to learn and grow more fully in the ways of God, Christ, and the Spirit?

Confirmands: I do.

Pastor (addressing the leaders [and mentors]): Do you desire to join with each other and with the confirmands to journey together in the Christian faith? Do you wish to learn and grow more fully in the ways of God, Christ, and the Spirit?

Leaders [and Mentors]: I do.

Pastor (addressing congregation): Will you, the people of [congregation] give your support to these sisters and brothers in Christ, to uphold them and encourage them in faith wherever possible, and keep them in your prayers?

Congregation: We will.

BLESSING

For this blessing, the leaders [and/or mentors] stand behind the confirmands, placing a hand on their shoulders. The pastor, deacon, or other worship leader approaches each confirmand and, in turn, makes a cross on the forehead (using oil to anoint each one, if desired) with the thumb, saying the following:

Pastor: [Name], by this sign of God's love, Christ will be your strength; let the Spirit guide you into the way of truth.

As the leaders [or mentors] continue to lay their hands on the confirmands, the confirmands pray the following:

Confirmands: May my ears be open to hear the voice of God; may my eyes be open to see the light of Christ; may my lips speak words of truth.

Leaders [or Mentors] (with hands still on confirmands' shoulders): May your shoulders bear the yoke of Christ; may your heart be filled with faith; may your feet follow in the way God has prepared for you.

Pastor: May the Spirit fill every part of you, and be with you in all you say and do. ·

Pastor (addressing the congregation): Let us pray.

Congregation (unison): Gracious God, you are the One in whom we live and move and have our being. Draw near to these persons who seek to grow in faith. Steadily increase in them, and in us, the desire to follow you, courage to question you, and willingness to learn from you. We ask this through Christ our Savior. Amen.

Pastor (to confirmands, leaders [and mentors]): The peace of God be with you.

Signs of peace may be exchanged. Confirmands and leaders [and mentors] reassume their places in the congregation.

1.   *United Church of Christ Book of Worship* (New York: United Church of Christ Office of Church Life and Leadership, 1986), 881. The English translation of The Apostles' Creed was prepared by the English Language Liturgical Consultation (ELLC), 1988. Used by permission.
2.   Ibid., 885. Approved by the Executive Council in 1981. Used by permission.
3.   Maynard Beemer et al., *Responsible Faith: A Course for Confirmation Education and the Rite of Confirmation* (Madison: Wisconsin Press, 1981), 29–30.

GLOSSARY

ACOLYTE. An attendant who assists in worship.

ADOPTIONISM. The teaching that Jesus was by birth only human and adopted by God as God's child at the time of Jesus' baptism. It is the opposite of incarnation.

ADORATION. To give honor, glory, and love to God.

ADULTERY. Unfaithfulness to the marriage vow.

ADVENT. The season of the church year that consists of the four Sundays before Christmas.

AFFIRM, AFFIRMATION. To confirm, ratify, or express agreement with and to be willing to assert this agreement with others.

AGAPE. The Greek word for love used in the New Testament for God's love and the way Christians love one another (1 Corinthians 13); God's love in Jesus Christ. Self-giving love, often distinguished from other Greek words for love: *eros* (longing, desire, erotic love) and *philia* (brotherly and sisterly love). The *agape* or feast of love was a common meal of early Christians (1 Corinthians 11:20).

AGNOSTICISM. From the Greek word *agnostos*: unknown or unknowable. A skepticism about or claim that God simply cannot be discovered or known by humans. Distinguished from atheism, which declares that God does not exist at all.

AIMLESSNESS. Having no aim or purpose.

ALMIGHTY. Having power over all; all-powerful.

ALPHA AND OMEGA. "A", the first letter of the Greek alphabet; omega, the first of a sequence or order (Ω), is the last letter of the Greek alphabet, like the English "z". "I am the Alpha and Omega, the first and the last, the beginning and the end" says the Lamb of God, Christ, who is coming soon (Revelation 22:13).

ALTAR. A raised structure used in the performance of religious rites in the Hebrew Scriptures for animal, grain, or incense offerings to God and in today's Christian church for the celebration of Holy Communion. Also called the communion table, Lord's table, or holy table.

AMEN. "So be it." A word used to express agreement.

ANGEL. A messenger of God.

ANOINT. To apply oil, ointment, or fragrances to the body. This was done in ancient times for a number of reasons: anointing the head as part of body care and cleansing (Matthew 6:17); anointing the head as a religious ceremony of initiation into the office of prophet, priest, or king (the title Messiah or Christ means the anointed one); a way of ministering to the wounded and the sick (Isaiah 1:6; Luke 10:34); a preparation of the dead for burial (Luke 23:56).

ANTHEM. A sacred composition for a choir, often with words from the Bible.

APOSTLE. One who is sent out to preach the gospel; a missionary.

APOSTLE'S CREED. A statement of faith from the early Christian church.

ASCENSION DAY. The fortieth day after Jesus' resurrection; commemorates the ascension into heaven (Acts 1:3–11).

ASH WEDNESDAY. The first day of Lent, so named because of a service in which ashes are placed on the forehead or back of the hand.

ASSOCIATION. A group of United Church of Christ congregations in a given area that organize for ministry and mission.

ATHEISM. A belief that there is no God. *See also* AGNOSTICISM.

ATONEMENT. "At-one-ment"; reconciliation between people and God through Christ.

BAPTISM. The sacrament through which God's grace, love, claim, and covenant are expressed to a person and through which that person is incorporated into Christ and the church. *See also* IMMERSION.

BEATITUDES. Blessings or statements about blessedness or happiness. Jesus's beatitudes are found in Matthew 5:3–12 and Luke 6:20–26.

BEGOTTEN. Brought into being, created.

BENEDICTION. From the Latin words *bene* (well) and *dicero* (to say). To praise, speak well, bless. The words spoken to a congregation at the end of a service of worship by the minister of God, or at other times when God's blessing is asked for.

BIBLE. The book made up of writings accepted by Christians as inspired by God and having divine authority; the Hebrew and early Christian Scriptures (also called the Old and New Testaments).

BIBLICAL CRITICISM. Critical judgment by biblical scholars based on the tools of analysis to find out as much as possible about Scripture. Not negative criticism, but constructive and challenging questions to get a clearer understanding of the meaning of Scripture, such as the following: What is the form and structure of the text? What kind of literature is it (history, story, laws, poetry, sayings, liturgy, legend, etc.)? Where does it fit in the whole book? Who wrote it and why? What was happening around that time? How did the first hearers understand it? What does it say to us in our day?

BLESS, BLESSING, BLESSED. The giving and receiving of God's good will and grace, bringing prosperity and happiness: long life, children, crops, herds, wisdom, righteousness, peace. Jesus spoke the blessings called Beatitudes (Matthew 5:2–12). The sign of blessing was often the laying on of hands (Matthew 19:15).

BODY OF CHRIST. A metaphor for the church found in the writings of the apostle Paul.

BUDGET. A plan of how much money is to be spent and for what purposes.

BULLETIN. A brief statement of the latest news; a regular publication of an organization; a worship bulletin.

CALL. A summons to a specific duty or vocation. In the church ministers are called to ministry in a community.

CATECHISM. Oral instruction—often using question, answer, correction—of those preparing for admission to church membership by learning the essentials of faith, discipline, and morals. These persons were called "catechumens" in the early church. The official manual for such instruction, such as the Heidelberg Catechism or the Evangelical Catechism.

CATHOLIC. Universal, applying to the whole Christian church. Sometimes used to mean Roman Catholic. See also ECUMENICAL and UNIVERSAL.

CHALICE. The cup used for wine in Holy Communion.

CHANCEL. The area surrounding the altar or communion table in a church.

CHOIR. An organized group of singers, usually in a church.

CHRIST. The Greek word for Messiah.

CHRISTIAN. A follower of Christ; one who accepts Christ as Savior and follows Jesus' teachings.

CHRISTIAN STORY. The whole faith tradition of the Christian people, however that is expressed or embodied.

CHURCH. The community of all believers in Christ; a body of believers holding the same beliefs and following the same practices, as in a denomination; often used incorrectly to refer to a building.

CHURCH YEAR. See LITURGICAL YEAR.

CLERGY. People who have been ordained to the ministry of Word and sacrament.

COMMANDMENT. An order; decisive declarations of God or Jesus, as in the Ten Commandments.

COMMISSION. An authorization to perform certain duties or take on certain powers. To authorize, empower, or give a commission.

COMMUNICANT. One who partakes of the sacrament of Holy Communion.

COMMUNION. A full spiritual relationship between people; participation in the sacrament of Holy Communion; a denomination.

CONCEIVED. Brought into life or existence.

CONFERENCE. A regional or state organization of United Church of Christ congregations.

CONFESSION. An admission of wrongdoing or sin; a statement of belief.

CONFIRMAND. A person preparing for the rite of confirmation.

CONFIRMATION. A rite of the church in which a person affirms his or her baptism. In many local churches, the rite of confirmation is preceded by a time of faith exploration and formation.

CONGREGATION. Christians in a local church when they are gathered for worship, education, mission, work, or deliberation.

CONGREGATIONAL. A form of church government in which the congregation is the basic unit of decision making.

CONGREGATIONAL CHRISTIAN CHURCHES. One of the two denominations that joined to form the United Church of Christ in 1957. *See also* EVANGELICAL AND REFORMED CHURCH.

CONSCIENCE. The sense or consciousness of right or wrong; an inner voice that impels us to do right in harmony with God's will.

CONSECRATE. To declare sacred or holy; to dedicate or set apart for the service or worship of God.

CONSISTORY. The governing body of a congregation; the church council.

COVENANT. A solemn agreement between two or more people; an agreement between God and people.

CREATION. The universe and everything in it.

CREED. A statement of belief.

CRUCIFIXION. A form of execution used by the Romans in the first century in which a criminal was nailed or bound by the wrists or hands and feet to a cross to die. The manner in which Jesus was put to death.

CUP, THE. The chalice; often used in place of the word *wine* in speaking of the communion elements.

DEACON. From the Greek word *diakonos*, literally a servant or one who waits on tables (Luke 17:8, 22:25–27). Jesus described his ministry as one who came not to be served, but to serve (Mark 10:45). In the early Christian community, the offices were ministries serving God and the brothers and sisters of the fellowship. Today a deacon is a lay minister who serves the church.

DEBTS. Often used in place of trespasses in the Prayer of Our Savior to mean sin or wrongdoings.

DEDICATE. To set apart to the service or the worship of God.

DEMON. A person or thing regarded as evil or cruel; an evil spirit.

DENOMINATION. A group of congregations that have the same beliefs and the same type of church government.

DEVIL. The personification of evil; an evil spirit.

DISCERNING, DISCERNMENT. Perceiving or recognizing, as in perceiving or recognizing the will of God.

DISCIPLE. The English form of the Latin *discipulus* (from *discere*, to learn); thus, a disciple is a learner, pupil, apprentice. The Jews were disciples of Moses (John 9:28); both John the Baptist and Jesus had disciples as followers. In the Gospels it refers to the large group of men and women who followed Jesus, including the Twelve.

DISCIPLESHIP. Being a disciple or follower of Christ.

DIVINE. Pertaining to God.

DOCETISM. A belief that Jesus Christ only seemed to be human but really wasn't.

DOXOLOGY. A hymn or chant in praise of God; frequently refers to the hymn beginning "Praise God from whom all blessings flow."

EASTER. The day on which we celebrate the resurrection of Christ.

ECCLESIASTICAL. Having to do with the church.

ECUMENICAL. Worldwide; a consciousness of belonging to the worldwide Christian fellowship. *See also* CATHOLIC and UNIVERSAL.

ELDER. An officer of the church who helps the pastor in caring for the spiritual life of the members. (In some congregations, this is the deacon's role.)

ELEMENTS. The bread and wine (or grape juice) used in Holy Communion.

EPIPHANY. The season of the church year that celebrates the coming of the Magi as the revelation of Christ to the Gentiles. It begins on January 6.

EROS. Greek word for longing, desire, erotic love. *See also* AGAPE and PHILIA.

ETERNAL LIFE. Continuing community with God in this life and after death.

EUCHARIST. From *eucharisita*, the giving of thanks. Holy Communion or the Sacrament of the Lord's Supper (1 Corinthians 11:20), which was the common meal, agape, commemorating the last supper of Jesus with his disciples.

EVANGELICAL. Contained in the four Gospels; a Protestant denomination holding certain beliefs.

EVANGELICAL AND REFORMED CHURCH. One of the two denominations that joined to form the United Church of Christ in 1957. *See also* CONGREGATIONAL CHRISTIAN CHURCHES.

EVANGELISM. Telling the good news of God's redeeming love in Christ.

EVIL. Morally bad; contrary to divine law.

FAITH. Belief and trust in God.

FAITH FORMATION. An intentional process of growth in faith.

FAMILY. Persons bound together by blood ties or mutual commitments that are sustained by shared memory and common hope.

FELLOWSHIP. Communion; an organization of Christians in the church.

FONT. The basin containing water for baptism.

FORGIVENESS. Forgiveness is God's word and act whereby we sinful humans are put into a true and right relationship to God; it is an act of grace, undeserved by us, a true gift to repentant sinners who trust God's promise in Jesus Christ. In the Bible there are many metaphors for forgiveness, such as: covering a blemish (Psalm 78:38), paying a debt (Luke 7:43), an act of healing (Psalm 103:3), forgetting iniquity (Jeremiah 31:34), a pardon (Isaiah 55:7), carrying away a burden, or being gracious. Repentance (conversion, turning) is required for forgiveness—not as merit, but in recognition that forgiveness is both needed and possible, and thus accepted.

FUNERAL. A service of worship remembering a person who has died.

GENERAL SYNOD. The national decision-making body of the United Church of Christ.

GLORY. Honor and praise given to God in worship.

GOOD FRIDAY. The Friday before Easter Sunday; marks the day when Jesus was crucified. It is called "good" because of the new life won for us in Jesus' death.

GOSPEL. The good news of God's love in Christ; one of the four New Testament books that deal with the life and teachings of Jesus.

GRACE. Divine mercy, love, and forgiveness, granted without any consideration of what one really deserves; a prayer of blessing or thanks offered at mealtime.

HALLOWED. Blessed; holy; to be held in reverence.

HEAVEN. Where God dwells; the fulfillment of life on earth.

HELL. The Anglo-Saxon word for the abode of the dead; the place of punishment for sin committed during life. Hell is a biblical symbol for judgment, condemnation, and punishment—not a geographical location.

HOLY COMMUNION. Another name for the Lord's Supper.

HOLY GHOST OR HOLY SPIRIT. The third Person of the Trinity who is ever-present to guide us in the way of God.

HYMN. A song of praise, adoration, or prayer to God.

IDOL. An image made to represent God and used as an object of worship.

IDOLATRY. Worship of an idol; excessive love or veneration for anything.

IMMANENT, IMMANENCE. Living, remaining, or operating within.

IMMERSION. Baptism by submerging a person in water.

IMPOSITION OF ASHES. Placing ashes on the forehead, often in a worship service on Ash Wednesday.

INCARNATION. The coming of God in the person of Jesus; becoming flesh or human. *See also* ADOPTIONISM.

INTERCESSION. A petition or entreaty on behalf of someone else; mediation; a prayer to God for another person.

INVOCATION. Calling on God, often at the beginning of a worship service.

JUSTICE. Fairness, righteousness, wholeness.

KINGDOM OF GOD. A way of life in which the rule of God as revealed in Jesus Christ is accepted. *See also* HEAVEN and REALM OF GOD.

KOINONIA. The Greek New Testament word for the communion, community, and communalism that Christians claim is unique because it comes from their common relationship to God in Christ. Paul often used it for the fellowship of grace and gospel; it is *agape* love shared. *See also* AGAPE.

LAITY. Literally means "the people" and usually refers to all church members except the ordained clergy.

LAST SUPPER. The meal Jesus shared with the disciples on the night before his death. Another name for the sacrament of Holy Communion.

LECTERN. A reading desk from which the Scriptures are read.

LECTIONARY. A prescribed schedule of weekly scripture readings.

LENT. The season of the church year leading up to Easter.

LITANY. A prayer in which invocations and supplications are read or sung with alternated responses by the congregation.

LITURGICAL COLORS. Colors associated with each season of the church year that are used in worship.

LITURGICAL YEAR. The seasons of the church year: Advent, Christmas, Epiphany, Lent, Easter, and Pentecost.

LITURGY. Forms or rituals for public worship.

LORD'S SUPPER. The sacrament instituted by Christ through which we remember Christ's life and death on the cross for us and through which we receive the promise of new life. *See also* HOLY COMMUNION.

MARTYR. A witness to Christ; one who voluntarily suffered death for refusing to renounce Christ.

MAUNDY THURSDAY. The Thursday before Good Friday. Maundy comes from the Latin *mandatum*, meaning command; it refers to Jesus' word the night of the Last Supper: "A new commandment I give you, that you love one another; even as I have loved you, that you also love one another" (John 13:34).

MENTOR. A wise and loyal advisor.

MERCY. Forgiveness; love that overlooks harm that has been done to one.

METAPHOR. A figure of speech in which one thing is compared to another by saying that one item actually is the other.

MINISTER. A Christian who serves, helps, gives, comforts, protects, shepherds. Also, a Christian set apart by ordination to preach the word, administer the sacraments, conduct worship, and do all of the above ministries too. One of the offices in the church—along with teachers, evangelists, elders, overseers—that is a translation of *diakonos* or deacon.

MINISTRY. The act of ministering or serving.

MISSION. The ministry of the church when directed toward others and the world.

MISSIONARY. One who is sent to preach the gospel, to teach, and to heal in the name of Christ.

NARTHEX. The part of the church that leads into the main part; the vestibule.

NAVE. The sanctuary; the part of the church where the people sit. *See also* SANCTUARY.

NEWNESS OF LIFE. A gift of God through Christ; the continual change of mind and action in accordance with God's will.

OMEGA. The first of a sequence or order (Ω) is the last letter of the Greek alphabet, like the English "z". (Alpha is the first letter of the Greek alphabet, "A".) "I am the Alpha and Omega, the first and the last, the beginning and the end" says the Lamb of God, Christ, who is coming soon (Revelation 22:13). *See also* ALPHA.

ORDAINED MINISTER. One authorized to conduct Christian worship, preach and teach the gospel, administer the sacraments, and exercise pastoral care and leadership.

OUR CHURCH'S WIDER MISSION (OCWM). The work the United Church of Christ does in the United States and throughout the world for which people in local churches contribute money.

PALM SUNDAY. The Sunday before Easter; the beginning of Holy Week commemorating the waving of palms and the subsequent betrayal and crucifixion of Christ. Also known as Passion Sunday.

PARABLE. A story that illustrates a moral or religious principle.

PARISH. Originally the geographical area and people belonging to one pastor and church, a portion of a diocese. Today, in Protestant churches, it means simply a local church community and its members.

PAROUSIA. The Greek word meaning the coming or the presence. Used in the New Testament for the coming (again) of Christ. It is part of the Christian confession about the end and purpose of the human story. "He shall come to judge the quick and the dead" (Acts 10:42 KJV, Apostles' Creed).

PASSION SUNDAY. *See* PALM SUNDAY.

PASSOVER. The greatest Hebrew festival. It became a memorial of Yahweh's deliverance of Israel from slavery in Egypt and the founding of the covenant. In the New

Testament and the Christian community, it became the background in time and meaning for the Last Supper, the death and resurrection of Christ as the liberator, and a new covenant with God.

PASTOR. The minister in charge of a congregation; from the Latin word meaning shepherd, therefore one who leads and takes care of the flock as a shepherd cares for sheep.

PEACE. In Greek and everyday American thought, peace is negative as "the absence or end of war." In the Bible, peace means what is affirmed by the Hebrew word shalom—wholeness, well-being, goodness that is free from misfortune, injustice, and violence. This tradition is reaffirmed by the New Testament where it is said of Christ, "He is our peace" (Ephesians 2:14–17). This peace is part of the meaning of love (Romans 12:28, 2 Corinthians 13:11).

PENTECOST. From the Greek meaning fiftieth day, because it is the fiftieth day, or seventh Sunday, after Easter, commemorating the events recorded in Acts 2 when the Holy Spirit came upon the early apostles. Sometimes called Whitsunday, a shortened form of white Sunday, for the white robes of those newly baptized during the festival.

PETITION. A request; that part of a prayer in which we ask God for something.

PHILIA. Greek word for brotherly and sisterly love. *See also* AGAPE and EROS.

PLURALISM. The quality or state of being more than only one of class or ethnic group; diversity and difference within a group; variety.

PRAYER. Speaking, listening, and responding to God either alone or with others.

PROPHET. One inspired by God to speak in God's name.

PROTESTANT. A person who belongs to one of the churches that has grown out of the Reformation begun by Luther, Zwingli, Calvin, and others; a protestor.

PROVIDENCE. Divine guidance or care. Another word for God.

PSALM. A sacred song or poem.

PULPIT. A raised platform, sometimes enclosed, where the minister stands while preaching.

QUICK, THE. The living; a phrase used in Acts 10:42 (KJV) and the Apostles' Creed.

RABBI. A Hebrew word meaning master or teacher.

REALM OF GOD. A way of life in which the rule of God as revealed in Jesus Christ is accepted. *See also* HEAVEN and KINGDOM OF GOD.

RECONCILIATION. Bringing back harmony after a misunderstanding; returning to community with God after sin has brought about separation.

REDEEMER. One who rescues or delivers another by paying the price; Christ, who rescues and delivers people from the slavery of sin.

REFORMATION. Changing into a new and improved form; the religious movement of the sixteenth century that reformed the church and resulted in the formation of various Protestant churches.

REPENTANCE. Feeling sorry for what one has done wrong and resolving to change one's life according to God's will. *See also* FORGIVENESS.

REREDOS. The screen or wall behind the altar of a church, made of wood, stone, or fabric and usually decorated with Christian symbols or images.

RESURRECTION. Being raised from death, as in Jesus' resurrection.

REVELATION. God's sharing of identity, will, and purpose.

REVISED COMMON LECTIONARY. A book containing a prescribed schedule of weekly scripture readings.

REVISION. A revised edition (as of the Bible); a new, improved, or up-to-date version.

RIGHTEOUS, RIGHTEOUSNESS. Doing that which is right; free from wrong or sin.

RIGHT HAND OF GOD. Biblically a position of honor and power in relation to God.

RITE. A ritual, or a prescribed form of conducting a religious ceremony, such as the rite of confirmation or marriage.

SABBATH. The seventh day of the week (Saturday) when the Hebrew people rested and worshiped God; used by Christians for Sunday.

SACRAMENT. A religious act and visible sign of God's grace and presence; baptism and Holy Communion, as instituted by Christ.

SACRED. Consecrated as being holy; set apart for the service and honor of God; dedicated and entitled to reverence and respect because of association with the divine; worthy of religious veneration. Holy in contrast to the profane and secular.

SACRIFICE. An offering to God; giving oneself for another, as in Christ's sacrifice to save all people.

SALVATION. The saving of people, especially our deliverance from sin through Christ's sacrifice; freedom from sin and community with God. The word literally means wholeness.

SANCTUARY. A place set aside and dedicated for the worship of God and therefore holy, such as the church sanctuary where the sanctus is said or sung. It also has the meaning of an asylum, a refuge, or a protected place where one is immune from the law in the presence of a higher law or authority.

SATAN. A name sometimes used in the Bible for the Devil, Demon, or the Adversary.

SCHISM. Church splitting; willfully separating oneself from the unity and community of the church to form a rival religious group.

SCRIPTURE(S). Sacred writings; the Bible.

SECULAR, SECULARISM. From the Latin *saeculum,* meaning "this age" or "the world"; worldliness. It is often used as the opposite of *the sacred* to indicate the difference between the church and the world.

SEMINARY. From the Latin *seminarium*. A professional school preparing men and women for ordination and service in the church.

SERMON. Proclamation of the Word of God; a discourse by a minister, based on a passage of scripture, for the purpose of religious instruction and inspiration.

SHALOM. Wholeness, health, justice, and peace. A shalom person is what the Bible means by the new person in Jesus Christ. A shalom society is what is envisioned by the rule of God bringing justice and righteousness.

SIN. Separation, being separated from God, from other people, from what is best in oneself.

SOUL. The essential self; the deep spirit in people.

SPIRIT. The breath of life; the soul; the Holy Spirit.

STATEMENT OF FAITH. The statement adopted by the United Church of Christ in 1959 and revised in 1977 and 1981 for use in worship and other settings as a testimony to the historic faith of the church.

STEWARDSHIP. The management of one's time, talents, and possessions in accordance with the will of God; thinking of all one has as a sacred trust to be used in service for God and humanity.

SYNAGOGUE. An assembly of Jewish persons for worship and religious study.

SYNOD. A church assembly or council, as in the United Church of Christ General Synod.

TEMPTATION. That which entices, especially to do evil; that by which one is tested or tried.

TESTAMENT. A solemn agreement or covenant; one of the two main divisions of the Bible—the one being the result of the covenant made between God and the Israelites on Mount Sinai; the other the result of the covenant made through Christ for all people.

THEOLOGY. Literally, "God talk"; the knowledge of God; the study of religion and religious ideas.

TITHE. A tenth part of something given as a contribution or tax for religious purposes—for example, giving ten percent of your annual income to the church.

TORAH. Law; commandment. Used as a title for the five books of Moses (Genesis, Exodus, Leviticus, Numbers, Deuteronomy), which contain the history of God's law for the children of Israel. An essential part of the covenant.

TRANSCENDENT, TRANSCENDENCE. Existing apart from the material universe.

TRANSLATION. Writings, such as the Bible, changed from one version or language into another.

TRESPASSES. Often used in place of *debts* in the Prayer of Our Savior; sin or wrongdoing.

TRINITY. God in three beings: God, Christ, and Holy Spirit (or Creator, Redeemer, and Sustainer). The Trinity is celebrated on the eighth Sunday after Easter in the liturgical year.

TRIUNE. Three in one; one God in three beings.

UNIVERSAL. Including all people on earth. *See also* CATHOLIC and ECUMENICAL.

VERSION. A particular translation of the Bible.

VISION. In the Bible, a vision is an ecstatic experience or dream in which new knowledge is revealed through something seen—whether experienced internally or externally.

VOCATION. A call to enter a certain career. The term is used more broadly in the church to mean a call to ministry and service in your particular occupation.

VOW. To make a solemn promise; to swear, pledge, consecrate—especially during a religious ceremony where a covenant is being affirmed, for example, marriage vows, confirmation vows, baptismal vows.

WAY, THE. The early Christians were sometimes called "people of the way" (Acts 19:23). They were followers of Jesus, who said, "I am the way, and the truth, and the life" (John 14:6).

WEDDING. The act of becoming married, the marriage ceremony and festivities.

WITNESS. A person who sees and can give a firsthand account of something.

WORD OF GOD. The truth of God revealed in the writings of the Bible, in Jesus Christ, and through the Holy Spirit.

WORSHIP. Honoring God; the act whereby believers enter into communion with God.

RELATED READING

Anderson, Yohann. *Songs*. San Anselmo, Calif.: Songs and Creations, 1978.

Bailey, Betty Jane, and J. Martin Bailey. *Youth Plan Worship*. New York: The Pilgrim Press, 1987.

Borg, Marcus. *Jesus: A New Vision*. San Francisco: HarperSan Francisco, 1993.

Browning, Robert L., and Roy A. Reed. *Models of Confirmation and Baptismal Affirmation*. Birmingham, Ala.: Religious Education Press, 1995.

Caldwell, Elizabeth Francis. *Come Unto Me: Rethinking the Sacraments for Children*. Cleveland, Ohio: United Church Press, 1996.

Coleman, Lyman. *Serendipity Youth Ministry Encyclopedia*. Littleton, Colo.: Serendipity House, 1985.

Confirming Our Faith: A Confirmation Resource for the United Church of Christ. New York: United Church Press, 1980.

Copenhaver, Martin B. *To Begin at the Beginning: An Introduction to the Christian Faith*. Cleveland, Ohio: The Pilgrim Press, 1994.

Davies, J. G., ed. *The Westminster Dictionary of Worship*. Philadelphia: Westminster Press, 1979.

Driver, Tom. *The Magic of Ritual: Our Need for Liberating Rites That Transform Our Lives and Our Communities*. San Francisco: HarperSan Francisco, 1991.

Dunn, David, et al., *A History of the Evangelical and Reformed Church*. Cleveland, Ohio: The Pilgrim Press, 1990.

Groome, Thomas H. *Christian Religious Education: Sharing Our Story and Vision*. San Francisco: Harper and Row, 1980.

————. *Sharing Faith: A Comprehensive Approach to Religious Education*. New York: HarperCollins, 1991.

Gunnemann, Louis H. *The Shaping of the UCC: An Essay in the History of American Christianity*. New York: The Pilgrim Press, 1977.

————. *United and Uniting: The Meaning of an Ecclesial Journey*. New York: The Pilgrim Press, 1987.

Hambrick-Stowe, Charles E., and Daniel L. Johnson, eds. *Theology and Identity: Traditions, Movements, and Polity in the United Church of Christ*. Cleveland, Ohio: The Pilgrim Press, 1990.

Hamilton, Virginia. *In the Beginning: Creation Stories from Around the World.* Orlando: Harcourt Brace Jovanovich, 1988.

Harris, Maria. *Fashion Me a People: Curriculum in the Church.* San Francisco: Harper and Row, 1988.

Hohenstein, Mary. *Games, Games, Games.* Minneapolis: Bethany House Publishers, 1980.

Holmes, Urban T., III. *Confirmation: The Celebration of Maturity in Christ.* New York: Seabury Press, 1975.

Imaging the Word: An Arts and Lectionary Resource. 3 vols. Cleveland, Ohio: United Church Press, 1994, 1995, 1996.

International Commission on English in the Liturgy. *Rite of Christian Initiation of Adults.* Collegeville, Minn.: The Liturgical Press, 1988.

Jones, Cheslyn, Geoffrey Wainwright, and Edward Yarnold, eds. *The Study of Liturgy.* New York: Oxford University Press, 1978.

Justice, Peace, and the Integrity of Creation. Geneva, Switzerland: World Council of Churches, 1990.

Kavanaugh, Aidan. *Confirmation: Origins and Reform.* New York: Pueblo Publishing Co., 1988.

Kispaugh, Charles, and Barbara Bruce. *Friends in Faith: Mentoring Youth in the Church.* Nashville: Discipleship Resources, 1993.

Make a World of Difference: Creative Activities for Global Learning. New York: Church World Service, The Office of Global Education, National Council of Churches, USA, 1989.

McCarthy, Scott. *Celebrating the Earth: An Earth-centered Theology of Worship with Blessings, Prayers, and Rituals.* San Jose: Resource Publications, 1987.

Miller, Allen O. *The United Church of Christ Statement of Faith: A Historical, Biblical, and Theological Perspective.* New York: United Church Press, 1990.

Monkres, Peter R., and R. Kenneth Ostermiller. *The Rite of Confirmation: Moments When Faith Is Strengthened.* Cleveland, Ohio: United Church Press, 1995.

More New Games! New York: Dolphin Books/Doubleday, 1981.

My Confirmation: A Guide for Confirmation Instruction. Rev. ed. Cleveland, Ohio: United Church Press, 1994.

Myers, William. *Becoming and Belonging: A Practical Design for Confirmation.* Cleveland, Ohio: United Church Press, 1994.

The New Century Hymnal. Cleveland, Ohio: The Pilgrim Press, 1995.

New Games Book. New York: Dolphin Books/Doubleday, 1976.

One Hundred and One Ways to Help Save the Earth. Washington: The Greenhouse Crisis Foundation (GCF) and the National Council of the Church of Christ (USA), 1990.

Reimer, Sandy, and Larry Reimer. *The Retreat Handbook*. Ridgefield, Conn.: Morehouse Publishing, 1987.

The Revised Common Lectionary. Nashville: Abingdon, 1992.

Roberts, William O., Jr. *Initiation to Adulthood: An Ancient Rite of Passage in Contemporary Form*. New York: The Pilgrim Press, 1982.

Schmemann, Alexander. *Liturgy and Life: Christian Development through Liturgical Experience*. New York: Department of Religious Education, Orthodox Church in America, 1974.

Shinn, Roger L. *Confessing Our Faith: An Interpretation of the Statement of Faith of the United Church of Christ*. Cleveland, Ohio: The Pilgrim Press, 1990.

Tirabassi, Maren C., and Kathy Wonson Eddy. *Gifts of Many Cultures: Worship Resources for the Global Community*. Cleveland, Ohio: United Church Press, 1995.

Trimmer, Edward A. *Youth Ministries Handbook*. Nashville: Abingdon, 1994.

United Church of Christ Book of Worship. New York: UCC Office for Church Life and Leadership, 1986.

von Rohr, John. *The Shaping of American Congregationalism, 1620–1957*. Cleveland, Ohio: The Pilgrim Press, 1992.

Walker, Williston. *The Creeds and Platforms of Congregationalism*. Cleveland, Ohio: The Pilgrim Press, 1990.

Weinstein, Matt, and Joel Goodman. *Playfair*. San Luis Obispo: Impact Publishers, 1988.

Westerhoff, John. *Will Our Children Have Faith: Bringing Up Children in the Christian Faith*. Minneapolis: Winston Press, 1980.

Wezeman, Phyllis Vos. *Peacemaking Creatively through the Arts: A Handbook of Educational Activities and Experiences for Children*. Brea, Calif.: Educational Ministries, 1990.

White, James F. *Introduction to Christian Worship*. Nashville: Abingdon, 1990.

———. *Sacraments as God's Self-Giving*. Nashville: Abingdon, 1983.

Yarnold, E. *The Awe Inspiring Rites of Initiation: Baptismal Homilies of the Fourth Century*. St. Paul, Minn.: Slough, 1972.

Zikmund, Barbara Brown. *Hidden Histories in the United Church of Christ*. 2 vols. New York: The Pilgrim Press, 1984, 1987.